16th & Bryant

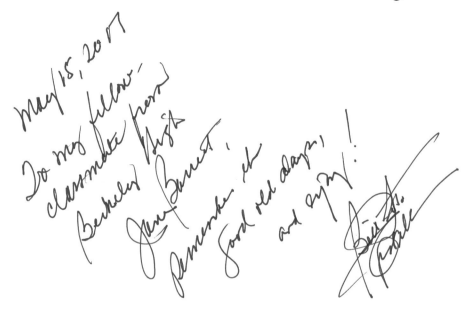

May 15, 20 07
To my fellow
classmate from
Berkeley High
Jane Bennett,
Remember the
good old days,
and enjoy!

In the long history of professional baseball on the
West Coast encompassing over 25 teams, 16th & Bryant
is the only book written by a PCL employee.

16th & Bryant

My Life and Education with the San Francisco Seals

Bill Soto-Castellanos

Clubhouse Publishing
Pinole, CA

Photo Credits:

   Dick Dobbins, The Dick Dobbins Collection, courtesy of Judy Peterson Dobbins: 41, 43, 44, 48, 50, 51,115, 118, 169, 180

   The Doug McWilliams Collection: 1, 3, 14, 17, 23, 31, 37, 56, 69, 71, 74, 85, 103, 107, 108, 116, 132, 143, 148, 151, 180, 186

   Photography by Doug McWilliams: 28, 29, 55, 62, 96

   H. J. Brunnier Associates: 21, 88-89

   Mark Macrae Collection: 18, 107, 138

   San Francisco Public Library: 27, 33, 35

   Bill Soto-Castellanos Collection: 45, 77, 80, 83, 158

   Zuma Press: 7

Editor: Jannie Dresser

Book design and production: Margaret Copeland, Terragrafix.com

Printing: Minuteman Press
         Berkeley, CA
         www.e-minutemanpress.com

Revised Edition 2017

ISBN No. 978-0-9786517-4-9

Manufactured in the United States of America

To order books: email ClubhouseBill@gmail.com

DEDICATION

*To Alicia Corella, my late wife of 57 years
who taught me that Love is everlasting,
our grandson Luis Antonio Castellanos-Perez,
our daughter Gina Monique Castellanos-Perez,
and all of the families of the men and women
described in the chapters that follow, this book
and the memories shared, are dedicated to you.*

Table of Contents

Acknowledgments

In attempting to travel back into time, all the way to 1950 when my life would change for the better, I relied on something I always had: a pretty good recollection of what was. I was motivated by two events, the Ken Burns' documentary film on baseball, and Dick Dobbins' book, *Nuggets on the Diamond*.

Ken Burns' excellent portrayal of America, baseball and its progress toward becoming our National Pastime moved me tremendously. Remembering Dick Dobbins wasn't difficult, not if you have the Berkeley High School yearbooks, the *Olla Podrida* of 1952. Dick was two years ahead of me and played Varsity football in games that were featured in the school paper, *the Berkeley Jacket*. Since I majored in vocational printing, I had something to do with its production.

Who knew that our paths would cross five years after he graduated from Berkeley High School? I recall letting him in the Visitors Clubhouse at Seals Stadium on an earth-shaken Friday night in March 1957. He knocked on the clubhouse door and asked if he could take a picture of Ted Williams. I asked the Red Sox trainer who gave his permission. That picture ended up in Dick's other book, *A Grand Minor League*.

After reading *Nuggets on the Diamond,* I started writing my first version of *16th & Bryant* on a computer purchased from my brother Mickey. When I went to work for SEIU in Marin County as a labor representative in 1993, I was required to work with a computer, so I had a few instructional sessions and found time to begin a serious effort to put this book together. I got overly enthusiastic and tried to merge photos into the text. After failing miserably, I dropped the project and gathered my wits. I continued hesitantly without the pictures and banged out a rough manuscript. Rough it was. I was all over the lot. I didn't work from notes but instead relied on what I remembered from 1950 through September 15, 1957. I saved all of my check stubs from the years I worked for the Seals and had a few group pictures. Unfortunately, I never made it into any group pictures, so you'll have to trust me when I say that I worked for the Seals.

As I struggled to write my book, I ran across the name of Doug McWilliams in late 2002. I wrote to him and we met at his Berkeley home where he showed me part of his vast collection of Oaks and Seals memorabilia. I saw and learned much more than I bargained for. Then he showed me the 1947 Seals yearbook; it reminded me of the copy in my possession inscribed by first baseman Bill Matheson. On the inside cover, Matheson had written: "To Billy 'Seals' Soto, a real Seals fan, from all of the San Francisco Seals." That's when I knew that I could write this book. Doug had all of the Seals Scorebooks covering the period of my employment and that's not all. He had the club rosters of all eight Pacific Coast League teams, statistical analysis of each year and related material. I had the check stubs confirming where I was during each season, all of my high school report cards, everything that would confirm where I was during the 1950s. I also had the check stubs and income tax returns that confirmed my various part-time jobs which augmented my life and education with the Seals.

The more I looked at the copied pages from the scorebooks the more I realized that with Doug's help, I could write something interesting. I was wrong! For several more years, I drafted thirteen chapters and included considerable references to numbers: hits, runs, wins and losses, and placements in the standings. I depended on Copy Central in El Cerrito for two copies of the bound manuscript and Doug and I read it and wept. I found the three years of work uninspiring and boring. Doug said it best: it's a repetition of what's already out there. The draft manuscript contained too many statistics. The same information could be found in other publications on the same subject matter.

I placed a copy on the table with other memorabilia at the Annual luncheon of the Berkeley Senior Yellow Jackets and I don't recall anyone looking at it. One of my fellow classmates did: Fritz Stern.

I first met Stern in late January of 1949 when he had recently graduated from Washington Elementary School and was in the seventh grade with me at Burbank Junior High School. At the reunion, Stern asked me about the book and said that if I was serious, he could make arrangements with a publisher. I mentioned this to Doug who encouraged me to write about what I saw and heard working for the Seals, that this would be what readers would find interesting.

Again, I put together a chapter, printed it and gave Doug a copy. He wasn't bashful, and so began the long, arduous working relationship where I learned so much about the necessity for accuracy. In addition to being a professional photographer who specialized in baseball, he was every bit a student of the game. An avid collector with a better understanding of English grammar, we became an interesting team.

By the end of the 2005 I mailed a chapter to Fritz Stern for his take on the effort. He liked it enough to send it on to Fred Fassett, publisher for General Printing who sent it on to Margaret Copeland, graphic artist. Her comments were encouraging and so I gave it my best effort. Completing our team Fred hired Jannie Dresser, editor, and this combination of professionals exceeded my expectations. I wrote it as if I were talking to you at a coffee table in your kitchen. I did not economize on the number of words; the words came out in abundance. Retracing my life for those seven years, from high school to after school, before and after each season, I discovered that I had received an invaluable education. Much of what I felt about the goodness of people began in West Berkeley and matured in the confines of an Emerald Cathedral, Seals Stadium.

A good example of this would be the pictures and other graphics contained in the fifteen chapters. They came from the collections of the late Dick Dobbins, courtesy of his widow, Judy, as well as from Doug McWilliams, the San Francisco Public Library, and H. J. Brunnier, Structural Engineers. Michael Davies, principal of the firm, graciously provided me with copies of the original architectural drawing. These revealed some interesting details.

Several members of the San Francisco Seals kindly resurrected some information that either confirmed or strengthened my research and (hopefully) minimized the number of mistakes. Assistant trainer Don Rode and former usherette, Marie Snead-Stanfel, contributed their recollections of the 1950s at Steals Stadium. Two players came forward with their thoughts on the PCL of the 50's: pitcher Bud Watkins of the Sacramento Solons and second baseman Jim Moran of the San Francisco Seals. Jim and I renewed and strengthened our friendship that began on March 16, 1951.

In my excitement of being an employee of the Seals organization, I almost forgot a story within a story. Eight clubs comprised the Pacific Coast League. Doug McWilliams and Mark Macrae have shared with me considerable information on the league's players, coaches, managers, umpires, trainers, and fans. They traveled to each of the eight cities of the old PCL and talked with those who remembered what it was like. They were kind enough to share their findings.

I thank all those who contributed to putting this book together. I found time to actively promote sales before the book's completion with continued assistance from my grandson, Luis-Antonio Castellanos Perez. He showed me how to put together the power-point presentation used in the promotional portion of this campaign. Finally, acknowledgement must go to all the players, trainers and umpires I worked with during those seven years, so long ago. Pacific Coast League baseball was enriched by their magnificent play.

1

Sound Advice from the Yankee Clipper

T he Great Mahatma of Baseball, Branch Rickey put it this way: "Luck is the residue of design." I may have had more than my share of good fortune. From childhood, up to and including most of my adult life, I have managed to grab my share of opportunities. Or, I might simply have been at the right place at the right time.

In late October 1950, I wrote a letter that changed my life. Addressed to Mr. Damon Miller, Secretary of the San Francisco Seals baseball club, it expressed my interest in any current or future batboy vacancies that the team might have. Two months later I received his answer. On March 16th, I was to report to Leo Hughes, the Seals trainer, for my assignment. I would be starting the 1951 season with the major-league exhibition games. Fifteen-years old, from a blue-collar neighborhood in West Berkeley just across the Bay from San Francisco, and I was going to become a batboy for the San Francisco Seals.

Fortune was smiling on me.

DAMON MILLER

I couldn't wait to get started but this new direction was still four months away. First, I would have to complete my last semester at Burbank Junior High School with passing grades. Winter came and went. By the first week in March, the local newspapers were beginning to report on activities at the Seals' training camp in Modesto. I read every article to familiarize myself with the rookies and veterans alike. I was practicing what I had learned in the Cub Scouts: "Always be prepared."

March 16th was a Friday game, the Annual *Call-Bulletin's* "Father and Son Night." Everyone expected a large crowd for the Seals' opening two-week exhibition series. They were scheduled to play the Pittsburgh Pirates, Chicago Cubs, New York Yankees, and Cleveland Indians. I took three guys from the neighborhood to my first game. Armstead Dorsey was a "Negro"—the word we used at the time.[1] My other two friends were Don Capellino and Rocci Giordano, both Italians. I am fourth-generation Mexican. Not knowing about "diversity," we were nevertheless a true representation of our ethnically mixed neighborhood. They had been my buddies since grammar school.

On that Friday afternoon after school, we boarded the University Avenue Key System bus around 3:45 p.m. It took us from West Berkeley to the connection with the yellow Key System F train on Shattuck Avenue. The F traveled across the Bay Bridge on a lower-deck rail line that rolled into the huge Transbay Terminal on Mission Street in San Francisco. From the terminal, we had to take two more buses on the City's MUNI system before reaching Seals Stadium at 16th & Bryant by 6 p.m.

We made our way to the right front entrance, the special gate used by the players and staff. Bill Wallace greeted us. He must have known that a new batboy was arriving that night. He didn't seem to worry that we were trying to sneak into the game. Majestically attired in a large blue overcoat that covered his towering frame, Bill had a big smile and a kind voice that welcomed us. He set the tone for what would follow.

I showed him Mr. Miller's confirmation letter and he led the four of us through the players' gate. At that point, he directed my classmates to the left-field bleachers, while I was shown to the walkway under the stadium grandstands which headed toward left field and the Seals Clubhouse. Bill told me to

---

[1]   The term Negro as used is not meant to be derogatory but serves only as a means of identifying persons of African ancestry. Over the next several decades this term was replaced by Colored, Black, and African-American. Persons of Hispanic ancestry were subsequently identified as Latinos, Latin-America, Mexicans, Mexican-Americans.

stop and ask an usherette if I got lost. I bid my friends goodbye and started off, following his instructions carefully. Except for a few ticket-takers and stadium staff, hardly anyone seemed to be around.

Alone, yet walking on air, I was about to go beneath the cement grandstands for the first time, even though I had been to Seals Stadium three times before. I trudged along the long wide ramp covered with roughly textured concrete then out onto the polished cement floor of the stadium concourse. On my way, I passed the Visitors Clubhouse and six stainless-steel concession stands lining both walls. A man and a woman wearing white and blue uniforms were getting ready for an onslaught of kids and adults.

I continued past the First-Aid Station located at the center of the stadium and past a concession complex. A young woman wearing a dark brown coat stopped and asked me if I was lost. I admitted that this was my first day of work and she kindly directed me to the first of two doors that led into the Seals Clubhouse.

It was the spring of 1951. Across the Pacific Ocean, a war raged in Korea. Many guys from my neighborhood—just a few years older than me—had already shipped out. In the fall, I would enter Berkeley High School. Whatever problems the world was experiencing, they took a back seat to my excitement about what lay ahead of me behind those closed doors. I was to be the batboy for the San Francisco Seals—a dream was becoming a reality. Although I did not know what I would be doing, I knew it was something that I had wanted to happen for a long time.

I was born in San Francisco, not far from where I found myself standing in the depths of Seals Stadium. In 1941, when I was almost five years old, my family had relocated to what locals call the East Bay. Returning now to San Francisco by way of 16th & Bryant seemed to be part of my teenaged idea of destiny. Five years earlier, I had been one of two kids in my neighborhood to win a baseball glove and a trip to Seals Stadium in a YMCA contest. (Joe Quiroz was the other winner.) One year after that—with a kind assist from my elementary school's playground director Carl Anaclerio—the Seals' first baseman, Bill Matheson, signed the inside cover of my 1947 Seals yearbook. He wrote:

Outfielder/First baseman Bill Matheson

3

"To Billy 'Seals' Soto, a real Seals fan, from all of the San Francisco Seals." I was known as Billy 'Seals' Soto from then on.

I opened the first door, took two steps in, and saw a stairwell descending on the left side. There was another green door with a forbidding sign: "Positively No Admittance—Player Personnel Only." Here, I was greeted by Seals trainer, Leo "Doc" Hughes who I recognized from group portraits of the team in their yearbooks. Doc's engaging smile, dark curly hair, and deep steady voice put me at my ease. I told him why I was there. He smiled and yelled out for the assistant trainer Don Rode. While we waited, I looked around. A little sign was perched above the trainer's rubbing table: "You're through when you quit trying." The scent of rubbing oil blended with the sharp odor of chlorine rising from two stainless-steel whirlpool tubs. When the trainer's table was draped in a white sheet, Leo was ready for any player who needed a rubdown. Nearby, another smaller table was decked out with manicuring tools and elixirs meant to soothe the body's aches and pains. I could also see several large wooden cubicles against the four clubhouse walls. They stood six feet high and three feet wide and served as lockers. Another set of lockers stood back-to-back down the center aisle.

Don appeared and shook my hand, then told me to follow him. We walked past ten or twelve players seated along the bench in front of their lockers, and entered an adjoining room. It was spacious enough to hold several large storage trunks, bats, and a tall cabinet. This room functioned also as a laundry and had an electric washing machine and a large upright stainless-steel dryer. (The batboys used this room to change into our uniforms.)

Don had earned his way up into the clubhouse after four years as a batboy beginning in 1947. He was competent and comical, an accomplished magician who often entertained the guys in the clubhouse. Nearly six feet tall and muscular, Don was dressed in white pants, a white tee-shirt, and a dark blue Seals nylon jacket. I didn't know him from Adam, yet somehow I knew we would get along. He looked me over and reached into the trunk that held the uniforms. Out came the traveling gray Visitors' batboy jersey with 00 emblazoned on the back—the traditional uniform for the newest batboy. I immediately got dressed in my first baseball uniform: a navy-blue Seals cap, navy blue socks and belt, and a used clean sweatshirt with—of course—matching navy-blue sleeves. At 122 pounds and standing five feet five, I felt great!

Next, I met the other two batboys who both lived in San Francisco and attended schools there: Lou ("Buzzy") Casazza, number 77 went to Sacred Heart High School, and Bob Rodriguez, number 88 attended Balboa High School. We began a lively friendship. They were "veteran" batboys so they told me what I would be doing and gave me their best advice: hustle and enjoy the experience. We had separate and distinct duties: Buzzy was the Seals' batboy, Bobby was ballboy, and I was to be the Visitors' batboy. It would be my job to retrieve the bats for the four major league clubs and the seven other PCL teams that visited San Francisco for eighty-four home games at Seals Stadium.

Casazza was a blond Italian kid, slightly taller than me. He had a teasing sense of humor and had grown up in a neighborhood where that was how kids made friends; it seemed I had known him for a long time. Bob Rodriguez had dark brown hair and was taller than both of us. He introduced himself by telling me he was "Black Irish" and since I didn't know what that meant, he explained that he had both Irish and Spanish ancestors. I told them I was fourth-generation Mexican, born in the Mission District just over a mile from Seals Stadium, but that now I lived in West Berkeley.

During the games, our job was to retrieve all the bats and balls used by the players and to help out in the clubhouse. However, before each game began, it seemed we had more fun than hard work. We often made a contest out of catching foul balls off the screen and the glass backstop. The winner was supposed to get a prize but by midseason we had lost track of the score. During Seals batting practice—if we arrived early enough—we shagged flies in the outfield or fielded groundballs in the infield. Sometimes one of the professional ballplayers gave us pointers—a surefire way to feeling we were part of the team.

For the first three years that I worked as the Visitors' batboy and Seals' ballboy, Don Rode was my immediate supervisor. He inspired me with his impeccable clubhouse, which became my model when he assigned me to the Visitors Clubhouse one month into the 1954 season. Before every game, Don swept and mopped the locker room with Pine-Sol disinfectant and vacuumed the carpet in front of the lockers. He washed and dried the team's soiled sweatshirts, socks, and underwear. When done with those chores, he retrieved the dry-cleaned uniforms and hung each one up carefully on the right-hand side of a locker so that the numbers on the backside of the jerseys were displayed.

In this way, the players could easily identify their uniforms and locate their assigned locker. The caps were cocked precisely over the right-hand shoulder of each jersey. As a final touch, Don draped a pair of white sanitary socks over each player's freshly-shined shoes.

Don had shoe shining down to a science. He took care of over thirty pairs worn by the players as well as the shoes belonging to the manager and coach. First, he emptied two bottles of Shinola black liquid polish into a clean coffee can. Next, he took his position sitting astride the bench in front of each locker, a white towel tucked into his belt and draped from his waist down to cover both his legs. He applied the polish with a two-inch-wide paint brush. It took him less than an hour to polish every last pair and leave them with plenty of time to dry from the polish and the damp thick grass of the previous night's game.

After the shoe-shining ritual and other clubhouse tasks, Don set out on his regular jaunt to the Hirsch Concession Department. This was run by Bill and Jack Cassidy with supreme efficiency. Bill and Jack shared a curious sense of humor and often took advantage of Don's easygoing nature by trading barbs with him. I avoided getting involved in their fast-flying jovial repartees for fear I would never survive. When the silliness was released from their systems, they turned to the task at hand. Don ordered several cases of soft drinks along with a case of beer which we then hauled—along with several bags of crushed ice—back to the clubhouse soft-drink container.

Don maintained a horizontal storage box in front of the center set of lockers where he placed the iced Coca Cola, Seven-Up, Mission Orange Drink, and Hamm's beer. He also kept chewing gum, chewing tobacco, candy bars, and cigarettes which he sold to the players at a reasonable price. He posted a list with each player's name on it above the box and whenever a player took an item, he put a checkmark by his name. Don also made sandwiches for everybody in the clubhouse for the half-hour break between games on the Sunday doubleheaders. At the end of the Seals' homestand, Don totaled the charges so that each player could pay him. They usually threw in a well-deserved tip, giving Don a healthy payday at the end of a home series.

Before the start of the official season, I worked the two-week major league exhibition games. I got my start as a batboy for these special games. Because I served the visiting major league teams, I met ballplayers from both the American and National League clubs, including some who were already famous.

One unexpected encounter took place when the New York Yankees came to town. I'll never forget March 23, 1951.

Prior to the game, Yankees' shortstop, Gil McDougald, asked me to go down into the Visitors' dugout and get a ball signed by as many Yankee players as possible. He had probably promised an autographed ball to a local friend or fan. There were probably seven or eight players sitting in the dugout: Joe DiMaggio was at the far end.

I worked my way down the row and all the players complied until I got to the Yankee Clipper. Joe was seated on the bench. He took the ball and held it for a few seconds, then looked up at me. "Young man, you can get a whole lot more cooperation out of us if you learn to say please," was all he said.

The look in his eyes was daunting. Several seconds passed until I uttered a meek "Yes sir." In less than a minute, I had received an invaluable lesson. I clearly understood that he was trying to teach me something that would help me all my life. After I collected my wits, I remembered that at my age DiMaggio was a skinny kid getting his first shot as shortstop with the Seals during the 1932 season. I was a shortstop, too. I realized that even though we were at different stages in our lives—he was ending his career and was plagued by injuries while I was hoping to establish myself—we also had something in common.

The numbers we wore said it all: he was a Living Legend with that big number 5 on his back. I was the kid from West Berkeley wearing 00. I took his advice to heart and made it a point to improve my manners. Thus began my education at 16th & Bryant.

Joe DiMaggio, the Yankee Clipper

2

View from the Field

As a teenage ballplayer I thought I knew the game inside and out. But after getting into uniform and working out with the professionals, I discovered how little I actually knew. Baseball—I discovered—is an exact science, every move calculated for a specific purpose. Mysterious signals are given and received with conscientious execution. Slow and deliberate, baseball is the timeless contest between pitcher and batter. Commencing with my first season as the Visitors' batboy, I was enrolled in Baseball 101.

The Visitors' batboy station was an unmarked area five feet from the on-deck circle on the first-base side of the ballpark: the domain of the batter-in-waiting. The first row of box seats were only six feet away right next to the field. My job was to stay alert as I bent down on one knee and steadied myself to retrieve the bat once the hitter completed his mission.

The on-deck batter requires several feet of space around him to practice his swings. It is the batboy's job to ensure that he has enough room while avoiding getting crushed by a struck ball or flung bat. I had to be as keenly focused as any player, constantly scanning the batter and pitcher, and trying to "read" the pitcher and his signals.

Batters give the game their undivided attention. On a rare occasion, a player might engage in small talk with the batboy. I could be distracted by these brief exchanges or easily lose focus because of the young, attractive usherettes who walked up and down the aisles in their form-fitting skirts and blouses. But, the consequences of inattention were severe: caught off guard, I could easily be hit by a foul ball.

I enjoyed the fans—the noisy ones and those who watched the game in quiet rapt attention. My view from the field allowed me to observe people in the stands. Most were well-behaved and attentive; they knew when the umpires and players were not giving the game their all.

During my first season, it was not uncommon to see many empty seats. Television had recently entered our lives and not as many fans turned out. Declining attendance affected most teams throughout the country. On average, 2,000 to 3,000 fans attended each game in a stadium that could seat 20,000. Weekend games drew the largest crowds; on Saturdays and Sundays, anywhere from 8,000 to 15,000 might attend depending on who was on the opposing team.

I picked up many colorful expressions: "Shake yourself," "Let 'er flicker," and "Smooth like crap passing through a horn." I tried these little gems out on the guys in my neighborhood, at school, and on the playground. When I was with Don, Buzzy, and Bob, I felt free to use my new unrestricted vocabulary. But, when I was around the players, managers, and trainers, I felt I had to be careful. We weren't told how to speak or behave, necessarily; we just knew our place. Manners—good manners—were used at all times in the company of adults. At school, I didn't follow the same protocols of self-censorship; consequently, I received my share of verbal reprimands.

My first season consisted of 84 home games. Night games were held on Tuesday, Thursday, and Friday nights, while day games were scheduled on Wednesdays and Saturdays; doubleheaders were reserved for Sunday afternoons. For Wednesday games, which started at 2:15 p.m., I had to make arrangements to leave school early.

Fifteen miles and the San Francisco Bay separated West Berkeley from 16th Street in San Francisco. I didn't drive yet, so I had to be resourceful to get to the stadium on time. At first I took the Key System bus and the 'F' train then completed the journey on MUNI buses. It wasn't long before I was able to hitch a ride with Dick Larner, a player who lived in Berkeley. He was an exceptionally tall, right-handed pitcher, a twenty-six year old rookie who lived on University Avenue down the block from my junior high school. This arrangement worked briefly until Larner was optioned to another club during the first month of the season. Next, I made commute arrangements with other East Bay players.

The luckiest thing that happened that first season was the relationship I developed with second baseman Jim Moran. After Dick Larner left the team, Jim generously offered to drive me to the ballpark and back, picking me up in Emeryville. At age twenty-seven, he was in his third year in organized ball and had established himself with the Seals as a good hitter and infielder. Among his many accomplishments, Jim could drag bunt with the best of them and turn the double play as well. Management let him go early in the season. When he left the Seals to join the Oakland Oaks, I felt like I had lost a friend and looked forward to seeing him when his team came to the City.

From the East Bay end of the Bay Bridge, we could see the top half of Seals Stadium with its six light towers. We arrived at least three hours before a game. We hoisted ourselves onto the floor of the loading dock at the stadium and walked a short distance to the clubhouse. It didn't take long to change clothes and get on the field for pre-game workouts. After the games, I joined the players for my ride back. After many night games, I often arrived in Berkeley past midnight and had to walk home from the bus stop. In the silence of the night, I learned to whistle Broadway musical scores.

I never missed a day or night of work and avoided succumbing to colds, the flu, or other diseases. For night games, I bundled up by wearing two sets of sanitary socks and a choker over the sweatshirt. On *dreadfully* cold nights I borrowed a fur-lined jacket from a team member. Don't let anyone tell you that it didn't get cold and windy in America's finest ballpark. The legendary chill lived up to Mark Twain's famous dig that 'the coldest winter he ever had was a summer in San Francisco.' On misty nights when it didn't rain, you could see a silhouette of fine mist wafting down at an angle in front of the light towers. It was 'pretty as could be and colder than a well-digger's behind.' That's how infielder Ray Hamrick described it.

Public Address announcer Jack Rice set the tone for what we should wear. Just before games on cold evenings, he motioned me to come over, and strongly suggested that I remain near the lower part of the padded backstop where it was warmer. When the Seals were at bat I followed his advice. Before the home-plate umpire called off a game due to rain, I would try everything to make it through the night.

My supervisors, trainer Leo Hughes and assistant trainer Don Rode, were also supportive. One afternoon I limped into the clubhouse after a running accident at school. Leo noticed my bruised leg and suggested that I jump into the hot whirlpool. Afterwards, he rubbed down my legs for about fifteen minutes. Much to my delight the aches disappeared. Leo had a noticeable distortion in one arm, the residue of a youthful injury, yet that didn't hamper him or compromise his skill. With a resonant voice, he often asked me about school. He seemed satisfied with my vaguely accurate response.

Leo and I discovered that we both were originally from San Francisco's Mission District. I told him I was born at St. Luke's Hospital and lived at 24th and Treat streets until I was four. He played ball at a park on that corner before he went to work for the Mission Reds. He had been their clubhouse man's assistant. He asked about West Berkeley and I told him how I had become a Seals fan, even though I lived near to Oakland and was surrounded by Oaks loyalists. I told him how first baseman Bill Matheson had given me the name of Billy 'Seals' Soto.

Having Don Rode as my other supervisor was more play than work. If Don needed help in the clubhouse, the batboys pitched in. Most of the time, however, we got into our uniforms and high-tailed it onto the field. Don let us enjoy ourselves. When he finished his work ahead of schedule, he often joined us.

During pre-game batting practice, we spent as much time as we could in the outfield or infield. We had to be alert and ready for anything. Except for one incident, I mostly avoided injury. During one batting practice I went after a hard grounder hit by outfielder Bill McCawley; it landed on the foul side of third base, hit something, then bounced, slapping me on the side of my head. Bill yelled out across the field if I was all right. I nodded and returned to the infield, continuing as if nothing had happened. Out on the field for four seasons, that was the only time I was ever hit.

I wanted to be useful in the clubhouse. At Burbank Junior High School print shop, I printed sets of rosters that showed each player's name, position, and uniform number, and then brought them to 16th & Bryant. Leo, Don, and I cut up the rosters and placed each player's name in the upper part of the locker for snappy identification. A second copy was placed on the ends of the traveling duffel bags.

My assignments took me to both sides of the field: into the Seals and Visitors Clubhouses and dugouts which allowed me to get acquainted with all of the ballplayers that first season. I couldn't help but notice everything about these professional athletes. Their uniforms reflected the Fifties and were conservative in style. Form-fitting uniforms were at least a decade away. They wore below-the-knee pant legs tucked into long outer stockings over long white sanitary socks. Their shoes were black leather Wilson or Riddell (cleats) with fold-over tongues. The jerseys identified the team name on the front and the player's number on the back. The color of the caps usually matched the outer socks. A few players had two-inch-wide plastic liners in their caps to cushion a pitch to the head. The plastic helmet was a decade away.

I also paid close attention to how each player looked and how he interacted with his teammates and with players on the opposing team. Most men were in their twenties or thirties. They came to San Francisco from every part of the country: there were city slickers, country boys, and hard-working, blue collar men. Each had a unique talent. Every once in a while, a college graduate would join the team but mostly the players were regular men adjusting to changing times, rookies and veterans who worked alongside one another. Former major leaguers on the way down played with a few star-struck "phenoms" anxious to go up to the "Big Show." A majority of the PCL teams offered salaries equal to the major leagues in order to entice potential big league players to remain on the West Coast. This explained why so many players preferred to float from one PCL club to another.

Most of the players were native-born Americans of various ethnic extractions. There were a few non-native players who mostly came from south of the border and the Caribbean. All were in extraordinary physical condition. Home-town guys talked about fishing and hunting, going to the movies, raising children, while the visitors talked about the good restaurants in San Francisco, the International Settlement where they found exciting entertainment, and jazz joints downtown. They wanted to know what was playing at the Market Street movie houses and talked about seeing *On the Waterfront, A Place in the Sun,* and the big MGM musicals like *An American in Paris* or *The Toast of New Orleans.*

Many younger players were of draft age and might be called up at any time. The Cold War conflict in Korea was in its second year. Older players were veterans of the Big One—World War II. Their patriotism was palpable. In 1949 the Seals had barnstormed Japan and returned to the states full of pride. Jim Moran talked about the enthusiastic response that baseball had gotten in Japan, from both the Japanese hosts as well as from the troops serving under General Douglas MacArthur.

In this era, most players had a tobacco habit. They smoked cigars, cigarettes, or chewed tobacco. Not a few snuck off to the dugout between innings for a quick smoke. Many chewed gum. Card games and Cribbage were popular clubhouse pastimes. Most all enjoyed a beer after a winning game, and both clubhouse men made certain to have a couple of cases of Hamm's Beer on ice after the game. Don Rode had a radio in the clubhouse; once in a while he played music, something subtle as a backdrop to locker room discussions.

First Season Line-Up

There were over 300 players to come through Seals Stadium that first year I worked as the Visitors' batboy. The Seals used close to fifty players during their 1951 season, and because of my position, I met nearly all of the visiting team players as well. Among the Seals, there were far more players who caught my interest than I can adequately describe here, but some were truly memorable.

The Coach

My relationships with Seals' players began with Joe Sprinz, a coach who had several years in the big leagues and over ten years with the Seals. There was something about him that I found compelling. In his early forties, Joe was stern looking yet soft-spoken. With an occasional twinkle in his eyes, Joe commanded my respect and I played close attention to what he said and did.

Joe Sprinz, coach

He had once received notoriety for attempting to catch a baseball that had been dropped from a dirigible 500 feet overhead. The ball fell with such force that it broke through his glove and broke his jaw. Fortunately, he was already an established catcher by that point.

I met Joe in the clubhouse but got to know him on the field. He seemed to like me right away; after a short time, he nicknamed me 'Rizzuto.' I guess he thought I resembled the Yankee shortstop after watching me on the infield during Seals' batting practice. Usually during workout sessions before the major league exhibition games, I positioned myself in the outfield although I was really an infielder. Once as I cautiously approached the infield during these sessions, I heard Joe yell out, "Keep alert and watch the hitters in the batting cage."

After a brief time, I became addicted to the experience of the infield, the excitement and the risk. And, why not? Groundskeepers Harvey Spargo and Ralph "Shorty" Schurr kept the infield immaculate. It was so smooth the ball would rarely take a bad hop and cause bodily injury. Joe recognized I had potential. He spent time hitting me ground balls at various speeds and location. I loved it. He found time to improve my fielding abilities and offered advice. He was profoundly smart, a catcher who knew every aspect of the game. He worked the pitchers and the catchers and did his best to motivate the team during a difficult season. That first season, however, Joe's main job was to assist manager Frank 'Lefty' O'Doul in making the team competitive.

The Catchers

Nini Tornay and Ray Orteig—both right-handed catchers—were the first people you would have seen looking from behind the batting box out to the field. They did the grunt work for the pitchers. Tornay was a rookie who enjoyed a good movie and loved opera music. Thickly built, he was well suited for his occupation. Just twenty-two, this was his fourth year in baseball, his first with the Seals. His pleasant disposition made him an easy guy to like.

Ray had spent four years in the military. By 1951, he was in his tenth year in baseball and his fourth year with the Seals. He had established himself as a consistent hitter with lots of power. He was the strong silent type and a steady competitor. One of the most notable things he said came in the form of a response to the manager. We had been clobbered by the opposition. After the game, everyone was looking defeated; Lefty looked around at the dejected players and said, "It's time for everybody to get the red-ass!" Orteig immediately muttered, loud enough for most of us to hear. "And what about Thurman?" There was muffled laughter in the clubhouse including from Thurman—one of only two Negroes on the team. I'm sure he had heard his share of racial remarks by this time.

The Pitchers

Chet Johnson was a classic example of individuality. A veteran of fourteen years in the game—seven in the Pacific Coast League—Southpaw Chet had a slight drawl or twang and a certain funny-bone twist on the game. Born in Redmond, Washington, he was a comedian and prankster who left nothing to the imagination. After spending part of the season with the Seals, he was traded to Oakland. I knew him more directly by observing him in the on-deck-circle.

One particular game illustrates Chet's remarkable sense of timing. We were playing Sacramento. The Solons' leading hitter was first baseman Bob Boyd, the only Negro on their team so he stood out. He was giving everybody in the league—including Chet—anxiety fits. A lot of fans attending this afternoon game understood we were not doing well. Chet's frustration got the best of him. He threw a hard one at Boyd, hitting him squarely on top of his head. The ball caromed into the air beyond the box seats and six rows up on the first-base side. Boyd trotted off to first base as if nothing had happened and Johnson just stood on the mound for about fifteen seconds. He took his cap off, slammed his fist into his glove, and scampered off the diamond, past

O'Doul into the dugout and the clubhouse. From the mound to the clubhouse, he kept muttering, "Just what does it take to get Boyd out?"

Another interesting member of the team was right-handed veteran, Manny Perez. Perez was in his fourth season with the Seals, his sixth season in the PCL, and his eleventh year in organized ball. He was born in Texas and raised in Southern California. In the first month of the season, Manny pitched the team to its first victory after thirteen defeats. He wore glasses, was an impeccable dresser and a serious competitor. By the end of the season, he had pitched more than forty games. As a Mexican, I had a special fondness for Manny, one of the few Latinos in the entire PCL.

Southpaw Al Lien was one of the older guys on the team. At thirty-six, the starting left-hander was in his fifteenth year in organized ball and his eighth with the club. With graying blond hair, he still kept healthy pitching in forty games. When the pitchers took sprints in the outfield before the game he was right there chugging along.

Outfielders and Infielders

One player that first season gave me a specific assignment. Outfielder and first-baseman Joe Grace came into the back room of the clubhouse and noticed that I was sitting on the large equipment trunk doing my homework. Joe was in his thirteenth year in the game, six in the major leagues. He could hit with the best of them and was good with the glove as well. The task he gave me took physical effort. I had to sand off the shellac on the impact surface of Joe's bats, then rub them on a large, clean beef bone with enough force to seal the grains, a procedure he called "boning" the bat. It required endurance and a steady hand. I finished the job at the end of the next two homestands. Joe thanked me and proceeded to lead the club in hitting with a .302 batting average. I allowed myself to believe I had something to do with his success.

When Jim Moran went to the Oakland Oaks, thirty-four year old veteran Dario Lodigiani filled in at second base. Dario was a Bay Area fixture having played six years with the Oaks. Short in stature, he had a body made healthy with good Italian food and was a strong competitor. He broke in with Oakland in 1935 (the same year I was born) and knew baseball inside and out. Dario showed what he could do early in his career when he played six years in the big leagues with the old Philadelphia A's and the Chicago White Sox.

Ray Hamrick was another ex-Oak who played with the Seals during my first season. What a pistol! The former major league infielder was in his eleventh year in pro ball and considered super competitive. He was good-looking, daring and funny, an exuberant guy who was full of life and told great stories in his distinct southern drawl. He played shortstop, second base, third base, and pitched in two games; in short, he did whatever he was called to do. He knew a lot about the visiting ballplayers, what they liked and didn't like, and what could rattle their cages. He was a good glove-man and could hit with occasional power. I liked him for a lot of reasons; he made the game more exciting and he had come over from Oakland. The fact that he could make you laugh was an extra.

By 1951 the Seals fielded their first team with Negro players: center-fielder Bob Thurman and shortstop Barney Serrel. They brought skills they had developed in the Negro Leagues which more than qualified them for the toughness of the Pacific Coast League. Bob Thurman was an extraordinary athlete with muscle on top of muscle. At thirty-four, he was well established as an all-around power hitter before the New York Yankees signed him in 1949. Everybody watched him during batting practice. He would hit ropes into the deepest part of right field with several balls going into the bleachers. Almost everything he hit went directly into the wind, too. Down the right field line it was 350 feet from home plate to the fence and Bob wasn't pulling the ball. He carried himself well, wouldn't be intimidated, and moved about like a Nubian King, powerful and proud.

Bob Thurman, rightfielder

Except for the fact that he, too, had come up through the Negro leagues, infielder Barney Serrell was quite different from Thurman. This was his twelfth year in baseball, eleven of which had been in the Negro *and* Mexican Leagues. At the age of thirty-one, he was an outstanding athlete: slight, swift, and serious as he struggled to stay competitive. He wasn't overly excited about Seals Stadium. He liked the infield but bemoaned those far out fences in outfield. Lefty played him at first, second, and third base. He could turn the double play with the best of them and worked well with the prize from the Yankee organization: shortstop Jim Brideweser.

The Manager

The '51 season was far from typical. The last time the Seals fell to the bottom of the league had been way back in 1926. I was oblivious to statistics and records; I only saw the courageous efforts of everybody on the team. Perhaps I was too close to the action to know what was going on regarding the Big Picture Day. When it came time to shoot the team picture, Buzzy Casazza and I failed to get the message and were conspicuously absent when the group photos were published. However, there in the front row, bottom left, was number 88, Bob Rodriquez, who did a fine job of representing us.

Manager Lefty O'Doul was a living legend and brilliant in every phase of the game. This season commemorated his seventeenth year as a manager. Not only was he quick witted and a classy dresser, he was the greatest of storytellers. I introduced myself to him just before a Saturday afternoon game, April 7th to be exact. It was a beautiful spring day with many fans arriving early to get autographs.

As I walked down the third base foul line, I saw him standing silently. As he walked off towards the field, he looked down at me and said, "Hi there, kid." I looked up and seized the moment. I was the new batboy, I told him. He grabbed my hand and welcomed me to the team. I mumbled something about how I hoped I wouldn't bring the team bad luck. We had yet to win a game and were already two weeks into the season.

He assured me that it wasn't my fault, but that we had our work cut out for us. With that he returned to his job, and I to my duties, and on with the game.

Rogers Hornsby's Seattle Rainiers beat us that day, but for me April 7th was one more day that was notable for contributing to my ever-growing list of memorable moments.

With dwindling crowds as our witness, we lost the last two games of the season at a September 9th doubleheader with Sacramento. If we *had* beaten them, we might have made it out of the cellar and into seventh place. Instead, they beat us both games. For the first time since he had become manager,

Lefty had managed a team into the cellar. We didn't know it when we left the clubhouse that Sunday that it would be Lefty's swan song.

Paul Fagan fired him a month after the season ended. It's ironic since he had begun his seventeen years with the ballclub by winning the pennant in 1935.

Camera shy: Batboys Leroy "Buzzy" Casazza and Billy Soto.

3

Behold the
Emerald Cathedral

One night, with the permission of Leo Hughes and Don Rode, I slept over in the tiny enclave of the First-Aid Station. On many Friday nights thereafter, I had the same privilege. I felt a great reverence for Seals Stadium.

After the last fan had gone home and the last custodian had finished sweeping up, and after the players from both teams had departed, I was truly alone. On the advice of Chico Norton, who supervised the janitorial staff, I locked the First-Aid Station from the inside then tried to fall asleep on the single bed.

Awakened by MUNI buses or street cars rumbling down Bryant Street, I worked up the courage to unlock the door and slowly explore the darkened belly of the stadium. First, I headed up the tunnel that opened behind home plate. I traveled the walkway that had been filled with fans, vendors, and stadium staff only hours before. I looked at the darkened scoreboard, then up at those majestic light towers. It felt like walking on hallowed ground as I slowly returned to my sanctuary—not intimidated at all by the stadium's dark stillness.

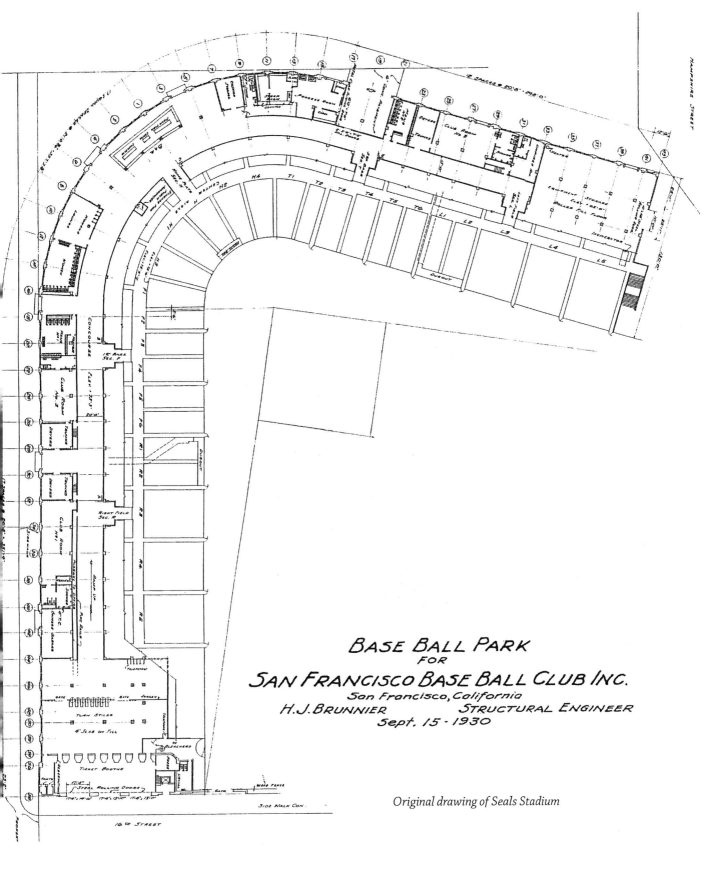

BASE BALL PARK
FOR
SAN FRANCISCO BASE BALL CLUB INC.
San Francisco, California
H.J. BRUNNIER *STRUCTURAL ENGINEER*
Sept. 15 - 1930

Original drawing of Seals Stadium

Seals Stadium was designed by H. J. Brunnier Associates, Structural Engineers. Completed during the Great Depression in 1931, it featured an elaborate system of underground pipes that provided good drainage and six huge light towers. When the towers were constructed and installed they made 16th & Bryant the best lighted stadium in the world, producing 115,500,000 candles-worth of power on the playing field: this was still six years before the first night game was ever played in the major leagues.

The playing field was larger than anything in the league. The outfield fences were placed far enough from home plate that it took a hefty swing to clear a ball over them. The unique feature of placing the fences so far out was probably the brainchild of owner Charlie Graham, a former catcher, who must have had the pitchers' survival in mind. Originally, the field's measurements were 420 feet down the center and 385 feet down the sides; this was shortened slightly so that the left and right field foul lines became 365 feet and 350 feet respectively (to make room for temporary bleachers), and from home plate to the scoreboard in centerfield was now 410 feet.

Enter This Way, Please

Take an imaginative tour with me through this architectural marvel. As we approach Seals Stadium's front entrance on 16th Street, we see a movie-house style marquee looming overhead; it announces the opposing team and the starting time of the game. It is visible to the people in Franklin Square Park and to the patrons of the Double Play Tavern across the street. Approaching the intersection, passengers on the electric street cars and city buses can also see which of the seven visiting ballclubs are in town that week.

Three metal roll-down gates stand below the marquee; these separate the outside world from the main entrance to the ballpark until it's time to play ball. On the right-hand side of the front gates, two glass doors open to an elevator that leads up to conference rooms and offices on the second and third floors. The stadium's address—2350—is visible above one doorway. The upstairs rooms were originally the general offices of the Seals and the other San Francisco ballclub, the Mission Reds. (On the third floor, there is a glass cabinet displaying framed pictures and historical documents, among them, a check dated in 1922, for $125,000 from the Chicago White Sox to Charles H. Graham to pay for infielder and hitting sensation Willie Kamm.)

Most fans enter the stadium through the front lobby where they buy their tickets from a row of windows along the west wall. The players and the press enjoy a separate gate to the right of the turnstiles through which they arrive.

A sports shop is recessed into the back wall of the lobby. Here, fans can purchase publications, baseballs, gloves, caps, and other souvenirs. A large indoor aquarium stands opposite the sports shop on the west wall where the team's mascot "Major," a seal pup, has plenty of room to move. Major got his name after a contest was held; it clearly reflected the high hopes and aspirations of fans, the staff, and the players alike.

A green four-foot high cyclone fence ran from left to right in the lobby. After purchasing their tickets in the lobby, fans proceed up a twenty-foot wide concrete ramp that has been grooved to provide traction for leather shoes. This passageway provides a gentle ascent for about ninety feet. Along the side walls there are open bays providing space where vendors rent seat cushions, offering fans an extra bit of comfort.

High above the ramp on the west side of the entrance, there is a five-foot wide catwalk that permits access to the general offices on one side and to the main concourse on the other. The first of the five vomitories is at the top of the ramp on the first-base side; it can release fans into the grandstands, box seats, and playing field. Straight ahead is the V-shaped main concourse. Its flat cement surface is tucked under the concrete seating structure. Several lights are suspended below the

Front doors to the central offices

underpinnings while other neon lights illuminate the stadium's entrance, ticket sales, and sports shop. As you continue into the concourse, you notice six indoor concession areas; they begin at the right-field corner and arc around to the left-field corner.

The first of three clubhouses is located opposite from the first opening onto the field. One is for the visiting team; another belongs to the Seals, and a third clubhouse once served the Mission Reds. Just opposite the Visitors Clubhouse is the first of six concession stands. These are done in stainless-steel and staffed by two employees, a man and woman in blue and white uniforms who served food and drinks.

The extraordinary women who formed the usherettes now use the luxurious third clubhouse as their private quarters. When the Missions Reds franchise moved to Hollywood in 1938—a result of the Great Depression and the City's inability to continue to support two teams—the third clubhouse remained empty until 1946. Then, the female ushers were hired and the space was redecorated with comfortable furniture, dining facilities, and ornate drapes—all replacing the wooden lockers.

The usherettes dress in tasteful and subtle color-coordinated uniforms including skirt and blouse, jacket, and heavier overcoat. They are prepared for whatever temperature might occur during day or night games. These are attractive women trained into quasi-military teams. The women cover their hair with berets, caps, or fedoras—whatever headgear is currently fashionable. They are led by captains and stationed throughout the stadium's expansive seating areas. It is their job to check tickets and direct fans to their seats.

The women's lounge stands next to the usherette's quarters. It bears an elegance that could compete with many luxurious hotels, restaurants, or theaters. The lounge features a pastel interior, carpeted floor, and elaborate well-lit mirrors and makeup tables. Women patrons can listen to the game on an upright radio while seated on fancy upholstered furniture if the game is taking place during an especially cold night. A lounge matron is on hand to respond to the women's needs.

Just across from the usherette's quarters is the first of two tiled men's rest rooms, built to provide the maximum amount of room. Originally, in 1931, there had also been an old-fashioned bar here to serve welcomed libations. According to architectural drawings, the bar was placed in the middle of the back wall at the center of the concourse. In 1947, Paul Fagan installed a shoe-shine stand for anyone who wanted to spiff up his or her looks.

There are two more of the six concessions stands located here as well. These offer a menu similar to all of the others. This is also where you would find the First-Aid Station, where I spent my nights alone in the stadium. During games, it is always staffed with a registered nurse who has access to medical supplies kept in wooden cabinets. The bed provides respite for sick or injured ballpark patrons.

Beyond the First-Aid Station, recessed into the north wall down the third-base side, is the concessions office managed by Bob Hirsh with his assistants, Jack and Bill Cassidy. They order and distribute all the food and drinks served to the crowds. Their office contains a large storage area, as well as refrigerated units, in addition to the necessary desks and cabinets.

Beyond the concession office, there are two doors that open onto a loading dock and a driveway that leads down to an unpaved lot used for parking by the players and clubhouse staff. If you walk past these doors and further down the hall, you would arrive at the first of two entrances to the Seals Clubhouse. The first entrance is used for deliveries of storage trunks, duffel bags, and equipment and leads into a storage room, complete with laundry facilities including an electric washing machine and a large metal gas dryer. When a team's trunks were delivered, they contained several sets of uniforms. A tall upright wooden cabinet holds bats, assorted equipment, and the trainers' supplies. This area also serves as the batboys' dressing room.

All three clubhouses are rectangular, measuring thirty-feet wide and at least one-hundred-feet long. The Visitors Clubhouse is a mirror-image floor plan from the one occupied by the Seals.

The clubhouses contain spacious lockers, showers, and rest rooms. Upon entering, you notice a long row of wooden lockers standing against one wall with a long continuous bench running before them. The manager's locker is located in the middle row between the two rows of lockers; it's large enough to hold a built-in desk. A telephone and desk reflect his authority. At the end of the lockers, a large gas heater hangs from the ceiling and provides warmth during cold San Francisco summer nights. There are also lockers on the north wall, and between the two rows of lockers are five more lockers positioned back-to-back in the middle of the room. A bat rack is stationed in front of this free-standing row of middle lockers. The lockers are painted mint green, as are the walls behind them.

The clubhouses feature three sets of tall windows of tempered glass against the back wall. There is a trainers' rubbing table at this end of the clubhouse where the trainer also has access to storage cabinets and wash basins with mirrors. Showers and toilets are located nearby. Across from the rest rooms, two stainless-steel, hydro-massage whirlpool tubs complete the state-of-the-art features of the Seals Clubhouse.

Upon entering the Seals Clubhouse, you would see jerseys hanging to the right of each locker, with the numbers displayed. Placed above the jerseys, are navy-blue Seals' caps with embossed SF lettering. A row of freshly polished baseball shoes parallel the lockers, with the traditional off-white sanitary socks draped over the bench. Sweat shirts and other apparel are properly hung while extra pairs of shoes and duffel bags are visible on the locker-room floor.

The black-and-white marble pattern of the clubhouse floor is created by the rubberized linoleum. The one-foot interlocking squares are covered by a light beige carpet that has been strategically placed in front of the lockers and along the major walking paths. You would also notice inverted garbage can lids filled with beige sand strategically placed around the room. These are for men with a fondness for chewing tobacco. There is also a large storage container for drinks kept on ice which is maintained by the clubhouse manager.

Next door to the Seals Clubhouse and across the hallway, is the dressing room for the umpires. These are relatively small quarters meant to accommodate three of the men in dark blue. They also have lockers, showers and restroom facilities and share the space with boxes of baseballs sufficient for the game. Opposite the Seals Clubhouse is the last indoor concession stand, convenient for players and staff alike.

The last door in the left-field corner leads to the groundskeeper's work area and quarters. A long wooden staircase leads down to the dirt floor below the cement seating area. There are several fenced areas for storing various sands and soils used in maintaining the field, along with landscaping supplies. A tiny shack in the corner serves as an office complete with telephone, file cabinet, and lockers. Storage for the portable batting cage and motorized equipment occupies the yard behind the cyclone fence next to the Seals' bull pen.

If you stood at the left corner of the field, you would have an expansive view of the playing surface. Both left and center field fences are twenty feet high and painted dark green. A twelve-inch yellow stripe painted on top of the fence dares balls to fly over. The scoreboard in center field, high atop the wall is operated manually by someone who stands inside and inserts the numbers, and electronically by the public address announcer as he records strikes, balls, outs and errors. The clock attached to the scoreboard has had its numbers removed and replaced with twelve letters that spell out SEALS STADIUM. The high quality sound system is one of the best in baseball.

From the outfield you can also view the complete structure of the stadium with its sixteen rows of lower box seats and twenty-six rows of grandstand seats. They are divided by a wide aisle that runs parallel to the field.

Groundskeepers Harvey Spargo and Ralph Schurr

The last row is elevated forty-six feet above the playing surface and 130 feet away from it. Custom box seating features movable wooden seats placed in partitioned sections.

Without a roof everyone has an unobstructed view. For convenient access to the stadium's facilities, five tunnels lead into the interior. There are an additional 2,000 seats in the right-field bleachers which were not installed until the 1946 season. Another set of restrooms and concession stands serves the bleacher set. A ten-foot fence made out of metal mesh in right field is rooted to a five-foot cement base; it permits an unobstructed view of the field as well.

Behind home plate, there is a large, curved, wire backstop that stretches towards first and third bases and features an unbreakable Plexiglas "window" to its half-way point. This was installed by Cobbledick and Higbee, a local glazier in 1947. Plexiglas also replaced the metal screens in front of both dugouts. These were kept immaculately clean to allow excellent visibility.

High atop the center rim of the stadium is the spacious press box that provided an optimum point from which to view the game to local and visiting reporters.

*Panoramic view of Seals Stadium
from the first-base vomitory*

For the first few years that I worked at Seals Stadium, I had to find a ride home after the games. If I failed to hitch a ride with an East Bay player, I depended on public transportation and had to make that long walk to the front gate. Along the way, I always glanced up at the overhead "courtesy" lights that illuminated the stadium's walkways. My route took me through one of the openings that led through the grandstands and out onto the playing field. (Called *vomitories* after the ancient Romans, these large passageways were designed to expeditiously empty large crowds from their coliseums and amphitheaters). As I made my way to the bus stop, I thought about all the fans, the players, and staff who had walked this same path for two decades. As I admired the various green hues and bright lights, I understood why the press had taken to calling Seals Stadium "The Queen of Green." In the depths of my soul, however, this would always be the Emerald Cathedral.

4

The People Who
Made It All Possible

We were a small army of nearly 200 dedicated to making Seals Stadium the best of all baseball parks. Each had a specific duty and responsibility.

The groundskeepers arrived first. On the nights when I slept over in the First-Aid Station, I usually woke up to see Harvey Spargo and Ralph Shorty Schurr walking by. Their jobs began before anyone else's. They were followed by Chico Norton, groundskeeper and custodian, and his platoon of janitors signed up from the Union Hall. It was the job of one of these three men to turn on the heating and cooling systems in order to have the place comfortable by game time.

The first order of business was to prepare the playing field. The groundskeepers fed and cut the grass field—considered to be the plushest in the league. Shorty rode atop a motorized scooter that pulled brushed mats behind it to sweep and smooth the infield into the finest playing surface. Harvey, Shorty, and Chico watered the entire field which gently sloped down past the chalk lines to allow drainage. After the meticulous performance of their tasks, these groundskeepers had every right to be proud of the field's condition. Eventually, I came to understand why they scolded the batboys when we played on the field before it was ready.

Chico and his janitorial crew swept and mopped the interior of the stadium. Several janitors swung large industrial mops and dragged galvanized steel buckets attached to wooden platforms on wheels. Others swept the stadium seating areas. They started at the outer rim of the stadium and worked down to the six-foot wide cement walkway that separated the grandstand from the box seats. Yet another crew swept and removed debris from the box seats down to the four-foot fence that separated the fans from the field. Janitors vacuumed the carpeted areas of all the offices and the women's lounge. For the most part, the work was done by members from locals of the Central Labor Council.

One journeyman electrician inspected and replaced burned-out bulbs in the light towers. Another made certain that all the neon and overhead interior lights functioned. His responsibilities included a check on all the indoor

Ralph "Shorty" Schurr, groundskeeper and companion

concession stations, rest rooms, and offices, as well as the exemplary public address system. Janitors double-checked the rest room facilities.

Shorty was responsible for making sure that the Plexiglas wall that rose behind the back stop and in front of the dugouts was clean, especially in inclement weather (always an issue in foggy San Francisco). This transparent acrylic shield was one more Fagan innovation.

Bob Hirsch, the concession department manager, and his assistants the Cassidy brothers, prepared their assignments for their employees. In 1945, owner Charlie Graham had given his business partner Paul Fagan the green light to revolutionize the sports world with a number of innovations. Among them were the indoor concessions stands where staff and workers hawked a variety of foods: peanuts, popcorn, hot dogs, hamburgers, soft drinks, beer, hot chili, bouillon soup, hot coffee, and ice cream bars.

Jack Rice, the public-address announcer, double-checked the electrical system, and checked the turntable that played pre-recorded music during the game whenever Art Weidner's band was unavailable. Rice also checked the scoreboard to make sure it was in working order. Since he had to announce each player, he always carried a tablet into the clubhouse, dugout, or onto the field, to write down the correct spellings and pronunciations of the players' names.

Don Rode and Frankie Donofrio, clubhouse men for the Seals and the visiting ballclubs, arrived at least four hours prior to game time. Sweeping, mopping, shining shoes, and taking care of the players' uniforms were just a few of their many tasks. Eddie Peguellian, manager of the cushion concession, raised the wooden hatches along the ramp leading into the stadium where mounds of three-inch thick cushions were stored. After the previous game, the cushions had been rounded up in a motorized carrier and returned. Middle-aged, reliable, and good-natured, Eddie performed several duties, including cooking for the second and third-floor dining facilities. He had a remarkably diligent work ethic.

Bill Wallace was the gatekeeper at the players' entrance, and Marie Snead was the box office cashier. Together, they assembled a cadre of ticket-takers who got assigned to several locations around the stadium. Captains Gladys Ferguson, Adrian Reulein, Ann Mahan, and Lila Wulff put together the usherettes' schedule and site assignments. Up until this era, ushers had always been older men. Fagan replaced then with smartly dressed, attractive and intelligent young women—a bold, historic, and popular decision that delighted the fans and the players. In their color-coordinated uniforms, they assisted fans in finding their seats.

The Pacific Coast League's first ever female ushers (usherettes) in front of the Seals dugout

The hometown team arrived three to four hours before a game for pre-game batting and infield practice. Some changed their clothes and headed straight for the trainer's table or the stainless-steel, hydro-massage whirlpools where they could treat any aches and pains. Other players spent pre-game time in the clubhouse, exchanging viewpoints on everything from baseball to the movies showing at local theaters. Meanwhile, the trainer and players from the visiting team began to arrive. Several sat in the box seats near their clubhouse to watch the home team work out and to admire the luxurious stadium.

The batboys arrived about this time—unless we had caught a ride with one of the players and come earlier. Under Don's supervision, we helped out in the clubhouse, then hurried out to the field to chase ground balls or shag flies in the outfield while the home team warmed up. When hometeam practice was over, we took the infield encouraged by coach Joe Sprinz. One catcher would assist Joe while a pitcher took position at third base. Buzzy Cassazza, Bob Rodriguez, and I held down the infield. We entertained the fans who showed their appreciation by applauding us for our efforts.

The three umpires arrived at least two hours prior to the game because they would need ample time to get into their traditional dark blue uniforms and catch up on changes in the teams' personnel. They regularly applied a layer of red clay dirt to three dozen baseballs, enough to supply most games, rubbing the shiny surface of the ball to prevent slippery deliveries by the pitchers. The umpires' locker room was next to the Seals Clubhouse which meant they shared the same tunnel to enter the field. Bob Rodriguez put the balls in a wooden container then placed this in a submerged receptacle near the end of the backstop.

Sportswriters from the *San Francisco Chronicle,* the *Call-Bulletin*, and the *San Francisco Examiner* arrived hoping for a visit with the managers before they took their place in the press box. James McKee, Bob Stevens, Prescott Sullivan, and Harry Borba all had extensive experience covering the Seals. They were joined by visiting reporters whose typewriters always generated several column inches in the next day's local and national newspapers. Press photographers took their positions along the edges of the field because photos too would be sent over the wire services.

The Seals' public relations director, Don Klein, began as a radio announcer but within a few years had progressed to being a television announcer. He joined the sportswriters in the press box. For years, Klein's was the face and voice describing the game for radio and TV audiences.

Gates opened about an hour and a half before the first pitch and the earliest fans went through the turnstiles into the stadium. Those who wanted to keep track of the score could purchase scorebooks from concessionaires for ten cents. Some fans used their time before the first pitch to visit the sports shop, while others—mesmerized by the sights and smells of the concessions—plunked down their twenty-five cents for a steamed hot dog and thirty-five cents for an ice-cold beer. A few autograph hounds made their way down through the stands to the dugout area where they might grab the attention of a player or two and get a signature on a ball or a program.

Teenagers and grade-school kids were among those who liked to collect autographs so they gathered as close to the dugouts as they could. Others positioned themselves in the left and right-field corners of the stadium where they waited patiently during batting practice to see if they might score a foul ball. Berkeley High School students, Dick Dobbins and Doug McWilliams, exercised their creativity by finding ways to take pictures of players warming up on the field.

Going to a baseball game in San Francisco was a special event. For first-time visitors, Seals Stadium and the fans themselves were a sight to behold. Women were smartly attired and prepared for changes in the weather. For night games, they brought sweaters, long coats, and blankets. High-heels clicked on the cement concourse, and some women even wore full-length gowns or formal skirts. Men dressed in slacks and sports coats and both genders wore hats throughout the 1950s. Some men wore suits and ties and had shoes shined to a high polish. The usherettes greeted all the guests and directed them to the seating area identified on the tickets. Fans brought the

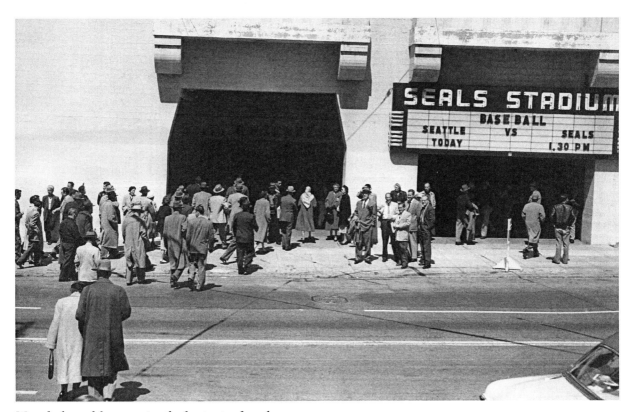

Warmly dressed fans entering the front gates for a day game

seat cushions they had rented from concessionaires as they made their way up the ramps and into their seats.

One-half hour before game time, Art Weidner and his six-member band positioned themselves on a platform above the tunnel behind home plate. They wore colorful uniforms to rouse the audience with John Phillips Sousa marches. A registered nurse made her way to the First-Aid Station and opened the door for an early arrival. In the women's lounge, a "matron" unlocked the door and waited on her first customers; she had already tuned the upright radio to a station that played pre-game music.

A contingent of San Francisco's finest arrived from the local precinct to ensure the safety and security of the patrons. Most of the policemen positioned themselves at strategic locations while some settled into their central command post next to the press box; from there, they had a panoramic view of the ballpark.

After both teams finished batting and infield practice, the groundskeepers returned the batting cage to the fenced area behind the Seals' bull pen. Next, they applied the final touches to the infield to ready it for the start of the game. The starting pitchers began to warm up.

Ten minutes to game time, Jack Rice clicked on the sound system and welcomed the fans. He announces the starting lineup. Next, the umpires enter the field to the traditional chorus of "boos" from the crowd. They are joined near home plate by both managers for a brief review of the ground rules. The starting lineup names are exchanged as the Seals take the field. The lead-off batter for the visiting team walks from the dugout toward home plate. Art Weidner's band plays the national anthem followed by the home-plate umpire yelling, "Play ball!"

In a deeply resonant voice Jack Rice began: "Now batting for Portland, Frankie Austin, shortstop, number 12." For the next two to three hours, Jack's voice was heard—not only in the stadium, but throughout the surrounding neighborhood. He rarely had to admonish a fan for getting out of hand. When a change occurred in the lineup, the home plate umpire walked over to the backstop and relayed the message to Jack who, in turn, informed the crowd. This was especially important for those who kept score.

The concession staff made their way through the grandstands and box seats proffering their goods, winding their ways around the policemen who were planted on the walkways. They were ready to make their presence known if necessary. If the crowd got upset with an umpire's decision, they might toss their seat cushions onto the field and interrupt the game. The home plate umpire would only continue when crowd order was restored and the cushions removed. The crowd hassled the opposing pitcher by taking out their handkerchiefs and waving them frantically toward the mound. This had been a successful strategy of Frank O'Doul. To the roaring delight of the fans, sometimes the maneuver worked.

Keeping with tradition, the fans all stood during the seventh-inning stretch. If the Seals were losing, some people began to leave. Most, however, stayed until the end even when the game went into extra innings. Pitchers threw at least seven innings, unless they were knocked out of the box; many completed entire games. (The era for bringing in closing pitchers was still several decades away.) Players also played the entire game unless they were injured. Pitchers hit for themselves or tried to. If a player was hit on the hand by a pitched ball, the trainer ran out of the dugout and applied ethyl chloride, a freezing medication that helped to relieve the pain.

Before the game wound down, the usherettes and the police took their positions near the fence in the front of the field. When the last out was made, both teams returned to their clubhouses to either

Concession Prices

Gaffney Red Hots	.25
Coffee	.15
Coca Cola	.15
Pepsi Cola	.15
Orange	.15
Root Beer	.15
Seven Up	.15
Butterburgers	.50
Ice Cream	.15
Popcorn	.15
Peanuts	.15
Western Beers	.35
Eastern Beers	.45
Chili Cone	.25
Score Cards	.10
Pencils	.05
Cigarettes (regular)	.25
Cigarettes (king size)	.30
RIO-TAN Cigars	.15

Ad from '51 Seals Scorebook

celebrate with a cold beer or sulk in silence. When permissible, the press entered the clubhouse to get comments from some of the players or the manager. Meanwhile, the clubhouse man was busy draping towels in front of each locker and already starting to work the dirt or mud off of the players' cleats.

Jack Rice, Bill Wallace, Marie Snead and her staff, Gladys Ferguson, and all the other captains closed up shop. Bill and Jack Cassidy tabulated their earnings from concession sales and took a quick inventory for the next day.

The fans exited across the field or trekked down the ramps even as the players headed for the showers and umpires retreated to their quarters for a shower and change of clothing. Trainers worked feverishly to relieve the aches from tired arms and legs of the pitchers. Depending on the outcome of the game, the manager either drank a few beers with his team or headed off to the showers, a change of clothing, and a quick departure.

A handful of fans often lingered near the clubhouse hoping to get autographs, and there were always a few players who accommodated their requests and answered their questions. Both clubhouses were nearly emptied by now, and only a few overhead lights remained burning. The gates in the outfield were closed and secured; the gates on 16th Street were preparing to roll shut. Players from the visiting team had made their way across the street and were enjoying a few beers at Stanfel's Double Play.

The janitors had their work to finish as they once again swept through the empty rows of seats. By now, the batboys had gathered up the bats and balls and returned them to the bat racks in the clubhouse. Then, we too changed our clothes and waited for our rides or our buses.

We went through these exercises for over one-hundred games in a season including the major league exhibition games. The people who made it all work were unique; they were members of a big league organization that had been wrapped in a minor league franchise with a designated Open Classification. That's above the AAA designation accorded to the American Association and the International Leagues and fractionally below major league status.

5

Those Men in their Traveling Grays

At the start of the 1951 season, I made it a point to know as much about the teams as I could although I was less familiar with the ballplayers on the opposing teams. The athletes that I read about or saw in games at Oaks Park were now the men with whom I worked. When they were in the on-deck circle, I paid attention and tried not to disturb them. During batting and infield practice, I observed, having sense enough not to invade the Visitors' infield since I could only work out with hometown players.

After each game I gathered the Visitors' bats in a large leather bag and hauled them to the dugout. Turning right, I ascended a sixty to seventy foot tunnel hauling over two dozen bats. I turned left, climbed eight stairs, and went through two doors. I had to catch my breath at some point in order to finish the task. At last, I dropped bats—ever so gently—into the bat-rack located in the middle of the clubhouse. Every so often, a visiting player lent me a hand, but mostly I was on my own. One unexpected benefit of this work is that I started to develop shoulder and back muscles, as well as muscles in my arms and legs.

Everyone from the seven Visiting PCL teams, including managers, coaches, trainers, and the players had something interesting about them. A few were extraordinary; most were ordinary men who were thoughtful and considerate.

Some were downright funny. Others exhibited an inspirational team loyalty. Few were prima donnas.

This was the Fifties. Americans were enjoying the benefits of thriving economy. In spite of racial and other differences, people generally felt they had unlimited opportunities. Many of the men I met in Seals Stadium had escaped poor neighborhoods by perfecting their skills in the minor leagues which brought them into the PCL. They conducted themselves admirably.

Neatness was in. A lot of the values and behaviors had evolved during the war years and a number of the players had trained as soldiers and returned from military service with a better appreciation of life and a strong sense of duty and discipline. This translated into signs of maturity exhibited between the chalk lines. Of course, there were those who lost their tempers in the heat of battle during a season of 180 games . . . that's part of the game.

The civil rights movement for equality was fermenting during this period as well. It challenged everything about America, including the game of baseball. If it was truly America's national sport, why couldn't any player take part if he had the talent and skill? At the time I became part of the PCL, it was in its fourth year of racial and ethnic diversity. Fierce competition in America's Pastime was forcing team owners and managers to focus more on performance irregardless of nationality, ethnicity, creed, or skin color. Some ballplayers may have had difficulty playing on mixed-race teams, but for the most part, once a player's ability showed itself, they came around.

Ballplayers expressed themselves and exhibited their status in the clothes they wore. Most wore slacks and a sports coat over a short sleeve shirt. They were impeccably dressed and clean, yet casual when they were off the diamond. Occasionally, a ballplayer arrived at the park wearing a formal suit, but casual attire was the norm. Leather shoes were polished to high luster with spit shine. Visiting players entered the clubhouse and changed into their traveling gray uniforms. Then, it was down to business.

The 1951 home opener on April 3rd was the first of a three-game series against the Portland Beavers. It happened on a Tuesday night with a crowd of almost 10,000 fans who showed for their first glimpse of that season's Seals. Bill Sweeney, the graying red-headed Irishman with an engaging smile, was the manager and he brought in a ballclub full of spirit to give the Seals a hard time. The first time I crossed paths with Sweeney, he complimented my work but I saw that he was tough on his players when they needed it and used whatever language or technique it took to get the most out of any struggling athlete. He had a rich mix of players from different backgrounds which brought excitement to the game.

Right-fielder Joe Brovia was a favorite with the fans and the press. Joe was returning to San Francisco, a place he knew well and loved best. For five years he played with the Seals, and then was traded by Paul Fagan because

Ex-seal Joe Brovia still a favorite of the local fans

he wore his pant legs down to his ankles. Joe was just fifty years ahead of his time. In his last season with the Seals, he batted .322. Brovia was anxious to take his revenge. He was an interesting looking man in his late twenties, tall and well-built; he had powerful arms ready to wreak havoc on the opposing pitcher. His batting stance was odd: he held the bat close to his chest and straight up. When he uncoiled, the quickness in how he attacked the ball sent line drives into the outfield. He spoke little in the on-deck circle; instead, he looked directly at the pitcher and studied every delivery, ready to attack the ball to the delight of the local fans who urged him on.

Second baseman Eddie Basinski was a work of art. Meticulously clean, he studied the violin and was at the same time a fierce competitor. He was one of the smoothest infielders in the league and executed precise double plays. At twenty-nine, the former National Leaguer was in his fifth season with Portland, an exceptional team player who could hit consistently. He conducted himself as if he was the captain.

Bill Sweeney's shortstop was the equally talented Frankie Austin from Panama, one of a handful of Latin-American ballplayers at the time. His presence gave fans a glimpse of the sport's future. Formerly a hero of the Negro Leagues, Austin was in his third season with the Beavers in 1951. Nearly thirty like Basinski, the pair worked double plays to perfection. Frankie was mild-mannered off the field, but with a bat in his hand, he was a force to be reckoned with.

Outfielder Brooks Holder was playing his last year. He was a sentimental favorite of fans on both sides of the Bay having played his first year with the Seals in 1935 and then several good seasons with the Oaks after the war. Before Portland, Holder had returned and spent another two seasons producing for the Seals. At thirty-seven he was going to go out in style and had returned to San Francisco to do just that. Friendly, quiet, and unassuming, Holder had good manners and reserve. Born in Rising Star, Texas, he had a natural drawl and filled the bill as a classic Southern Gentleman.

Marino "Chick" Pieretti went out of his way to make friends. The right-handed pitching sensation was originally from San Francisco. He assumed that I was Italian and I waited a long time to correct him. We both loved Mario Lanza and talked about his first movie, *That Midnight Kiss*. Somewhat small in stature but with a big heart, Pieretti enjoyed razzing me. When I finally told him I was Mexican, he said that was close enough to Italian.

Portland beat the Seals all three games—it wasn't a good start for the season.

After Wednesday's game, the Beavers pulled out and the Seattle Rainiers came in for a four-game series that launched on Thursday night. The Rainiers, managed by Hall-of-Famer Rogers Hornsby, were ready to inflict heavy damage.

Hornsby was quite a contrast after Sweeney. He said little and was not friendly, yet he certainly concentrated on producing a winning team. When I carried the bats back to the clubhouse after a game, I noticed that although the players were happy as hell, they were restrained in showing it. Hornsby must have been one hell of a ballplayer to make it into the Hall of Fame. My curiosity got the best of me. Rather than asking his players what they knew about their manager, I visited the West Berkeley Public Library.

Born in Texas, Hornsby began playing major league baseball at age nineteen. He was a consummate ballplayer and could run, hit, and field with the best. When I met him, he was already fifty-five and had been in organized ball for thirty-six years. He had seen the game he loved change in many ways. Coming from the south when he did, integration may have posed a challenge for him. Managing Jim Rivera may have even grated on him: Rogers was quiet and orderly while Jim was wild as one could be. As a major league manager, Hornsby eventually lost more games than he won. This was his first year managing in the PCL.

Rainiers outfielder Jimmy Rivera was swift on the base paths, a good fielder, and could hit with regularity. He ran the bases like his life depended on it and brought an exciting brand

Hall of Famer, Roger Hornsby

of baseball into the league. Of Puerto Rican ancestry, he had grown up on the East Coast, and came into the league prepared to make his mark. He said little in the on-deck circle and often gave me the impression that he was glaring at the pitchers. Tempestuous and determined, Riviera seemed to see himself as the Puerto Rican Ty Cobb.

Ex-major leaguers, infielder Walt Judnich and outfielder Al Lyons had established hitting reputations in the league. The PCL box scores and their statistics were printed in the yellow sports pages of the *Oakland Post-Enquirer*. At thirty-five, left-handed Judnich had power from the right side of the plate, while thirty-three year old Lyons would murder pitching from the left side. They were both built powerfully, each standing over six-feet tall and weighing over 200 pounds. They were a force to be reckoned with. Lyons also pitched. He had this thing of keeping the top button on his shirt unfastened while everyone else in San Francisco was buttoned-up. His enormous power parked one over the scoreboard at Seals Stadium which warranted a gold star that was painted on the exact spot where the ball left the park, better than 425 feet from home plate.

When Bob Hall stepped out of the dugout, he immediately got my attention. He was one of the team's right-handed pitchers. I was impressed by his demeanor and immaculate style: even in his baseball uniform he looked well-attired. While in the batter's on-deck circle, he chatted with me about the fans and the beautiful ballpark. I enjoyed his conversations with his teammates because he seemed to have an unlimited grasp of topical issues. I assumed he was well-educated.

George Vico possessed sheer grace with the glove and could do the splits while stretching for a throw to first base. Rough-and-tough looking, he was nevertheless kind and considerate to me and a favorite with the fans. George had been first baseman for the Detroit Tigers before joining the Rainiers. When he fielded short throws to the bag, he was a thing of beauty.

The four-game series with the Rainiers concluded with a Sunday doubleheader on April 15th before a sizeable crowd. It looked like Seattle was going to take

After thirteen losses, O'Doul kisses pitcher Manny Perez with Joe Sprinz and Dario Lodigiani looking on

four games in a row. O'Doul placed his hopes on right-handed pitcher Manny Perez for the second game, a smart move that led to a Seals win. There would be hoopin' and hollerin' in the clubhouse with beer for the players and soft drinks for the batboys. A newspaper photographer snapped O'Doul kissing Manny Perez on the cheek.

I had another reason to celebrate: I received my first pay check, over $20 for seven games! I hadn't even known that I was going to be paid! Mr. Miller had not mentioned money in his letter to me.

In the following week, I struggled to keep my focus on school. There were two more months before graduation from junior high school and I had my work cut out. That first check started me on a path of financial independence. I became less of a drain on my parents and started to spend my money as only a teenager can: I bought new gym shoes and school clothes in anticipation of my first year in high school.

From the author's vault

6

My New Life: First Season with the Seals

Frankie Jacobs was comical looking and spoke with a gruffness that was accentuated by the remains of a partially-eaten cigar that frequently stuck out of one side of his mouth. Once a boxer, he was now a somewhat elderly man dressed in white and standing no taller than five feet. Yet, he had a wild sense of humor and occasionally taunted me to "go a few rounds" with him. I was dumb, but not stupid; he would have wiped the clubhouse floor with me. His strong arms were attached to an even stronger body as he grabbed my hands with a strong grip: "You'd better hustle when you see me, kid."

Don Rode had told me that it was important to get along with the visiting trainers. I took Rode's and Jacob's advise to heart: get along with the visiting trainers and hustle when I see them coming. I got suited up and proceeded to do the best job I could working for the men in their traveling grays.

After the Seals lost to the Seattle Rainiers, they faced a four-game series with the Hollywood Stars. I managed to ride to the stadium for a short time with right-handed pitcher Dick Larner in his red Ford convertible. We talked about the Seals' difficulty putting together a winning streak and how everyone was doing their best for Lefty. Dick wasn't sure of his position with the club since the pitchers were all struggling to keep the ball in the park. Time would tell.

The Hollywood Stars rode into town with a real Hollywood movie star, Michael O'Shea. I met him in the dugout and found him talkative yet considerate. He loved baseball as much as I enjoyed the movies. I enjoyed hearing about his beautiful wife, the actress Virginia Mayo. One player teased O'Shea, wondering aloud why she would have married Michael. Pantomiming a scene from one of his Westerns, O'Shea pulled an invisible gun out of a non-existent holster and shot the culprit between his eyes! The players in the dugout all thought that was pretty funny.

Chuck Stevens was one of the most congenial fellows in the club. He was a left-handed first baseman, a fourteen-year veteran with a classy glove and skill at bat. When he saw me taking infield with the batboys, he suggested that I keep my eyes on the ball, ready to throw it to first base when I made contact with the glove. Pay attention to coach Joe Sprinz, he advised: "He knows what he's talking about."

The local fans' favorite was the former Seals outfielder, Dino Restelli, now playing with the Stars after having been picked up first by the Pittsburgh Pirates during the 1949 season. Two years later he was back with Pittsburgh's farm club in Hollywood. Local fans loved him no matter which team he was on. He had hit a homerun on the night of my first game in March and alternated with several other outfielders on a team that looked like they could win the pennant. He was good defensively with the glove and manager Fred Haney used him against left-handed pitchers.

Next, the Seals played a four-game series with their cross-bay rivals, the Oakland Oaks. The animosity that I had felt toward this club ceased when they ran down the tunnel onto the field. I had to treat them with the same respect and consideration that I gave the other teams. I knew almost everything about the Oaks. They were regularly featured in the sports pages of the local papers, and in Bud Foster's radio broadcasts. I collected some of their colorful baseball cards issued in the neighborhood grocery stores. I felt a little anxious to meet the players I had once rooted against but I swallowed my pride and walked quickly across the field, into the dugout, up the tunnel and into the Visitors Clubhouse.

Jesse "Red" Adams, the Oaks trainer, met me and I introduced myself by telling him that I was a classmate of two of his team's batboys, Leroy Lawrence and Howard Storm. Red knew the neighborhood I was from and described James Kenney Park with elaborate detail. He had wispy white hair, a twinkle in his eyes, and a charming smile. I could tell we would get along. When we shook hands, his firm grip made me want to bite my lip to keep from yelling. If he got mad at me for some silly thing I said or did, he would shake his head and give me a look like my mother sometimes gave me; it was partly a look of disgust. I worked extra hard when I was around Red.

The Oaks ballclub was managed by Mel Ott (formerly of the New York Giants) who succeeded Charlie Dressen; Dressen had managed the club to their second pennant in three years. Ott was a student of the game and had all the necessary credentials to motivate the team. He was rather plain looking, all business. An accomplished hitter and future member of the Hall of Fame, he helped the younger players at the same time he gave veteran players direction.

Longball-hitting outfielder, Earl Rapp

The Oaks outfielder Earl Rapp was classy with the bat, waiting for the right pitch until he attacked the ball with a well-timed and precise swing. The left-hander stood over six feet tall with a slender build. He could easily lace line drives into the outfield. Because of his power-hitting abilities, he commanded respect from the opposing pitchers. But he was also good with the glove and was valued as much for his defensive as his offensive playing. The thirty year old was in his fourth year in the league, his eighth year in professional ball after having spent three years in the military.

I felt I had something in common with third baseman Johnny "Spider" Jorgensen. The former third baseman with the Brooklyn Dodgers noticed me taking infield practice with the batboys. During the game he would tell me from the on-deck circle to keep my eyes on the ball. When balls were hit anywhere near third base, he came up with it and made the play. Standing next to him, I noticed he was slightly taller than me. The thirty-two year old veteran could hit with consistency so I kept my eyes on him whenever the Oaks came to town.

Augie Galan was another ex-Dodger on the team. He was a West Berkeley native. As a player-coach he filled in wherever the team needed him either in the outfield or infield. He left the Seals as their starting shortstop in 1933 to move into the major leagues with the Chicago Cubs. After eight years with the Cubs, he spent the next eight years with Brooklyn, Cincinnati, the New York Yankees and the Philadelphia A's. By every standard Augie possessed more than adequate credentials. Nearly forty years old, he was strikingly good-looking, full of life and anxious to help out his friend Brick Laws, the team's owner. Because he grew up near Kenney Park, he also used his talents to teach the neighborhood teenage ballplayers the fundamentals. Billy Martin was one of his prize pupils.

For sheer excitement there was nothing like shortstop Artie Wilson. Artie broke into the league in 1949, a thirty-one year old veteran from the Negro Leagues. He was all hustle, as good with the bat as with the glove. He led the league in stolen bases during his first two years. His was the voice you heard above the other infielders, yelling support to his pitcher. He studied every aspect of every move of the opposing pitcher.

Playing in his first year in the league was jack-of-all-trades, Lorenzo "Piper" Davis. Piper established himself as an all-around player in the Negro Leagues. In 1950 he was the first Negro to sign a contract with the Boston Red Sox. When he was thirty-four, he came to the Oaks fully prepared to play. Manager Mel Ott placed him in both the outfield and infield. He had intense concentration in the on-deck circle and spoke little to anyone near him. I remember watching him lean forward on one knee as he stared at the pitcher, hoping to pick up something in the ball's delivery, something in the way the pitcher held the ball. He looked for anything that would give him the edge when it was his turn at bat.

The Seals spent the week of April 24th traveling to Portland for three games and to Seattle for four games. They returned on May 1st for a three-game series with the Los Angeles Angels, our rivals from the south. From the beginning of the league in 1903, Los Angeles and San Francisco accounted for almost twenty championships. Both teams had the finest ballparks in the league: Wrigley Field and Seals Stadium.

Among the ballplayers manager Stan Hack brought to 16th & Bryant, three stood out. The Angels brought Hollywood actor Chuck Connors who played first base. He was a character in every sense. He was a good glove man and could hit with power. In his late twenties, he was rugged looking with an engaging smile. He played the role of villain well when he belted one over the right-field bleachers. A gold star was painted on the back wall above the bleachers after he hit the ball hard enough to send it 385 feet to the wall then another 20 feet over the back wall. It landed on 16th Street in front of Franklin Square.

Film actor Chuck Connors

The Angels also had one of the best fielding short-stops in the league: twenty-six year old Gene Baker, in his second season with the club. A former member of the Kansas City Monarchs of the Negro Leagues, Baker was signed by the Chicago Cubs and sent down to Los Angeles. At twenty-six, he was the only Negro on his team. Gene was considered by many as the best fielding short-stop in baseball, second only to Ernie Banks of the Cubs. His remarkable defensive skills coupled with a steady bat and swiftness on the base paths made him a "triple threat."

I had heard so much about outfielder Max West that it was a treat to meet him. He started his career in baseball in 1935 with the Sacramento Solons. He was a left-hand-ed power hitter. At Oaks Park he sent balls scorching into the right-field bleachers. At thirty-five, this was his four-teenth year in baseball; he spent seven of them in the major leagues and seven in the PCL. He played in Seals Stadium in 1936 with the Mission Reds, when the right-field fence was still 385 feet from home plate (before bleachers were installed and some of the distance was shaved off). Max West was a living legend to me and I just watched and listened when he was in the on-deck circle.

The Angels were a fun-loving club, full of bravado and a need to produce for their manager, Stan Hack. Hack served as a third baseman with the Chicago Cubs and had a positive sense about himself and his team. Their relaxed behavior translated into a highly competitive ballclub. The next five months would determine if they could improve over their seventh place finish the year before.

After the Angels left town, the Seals took off for a weekend series with the Sacramento Solons, returning Tuesday, May 8th, for a three-game series with the San Diego Padres. Managed by Del Baker and coached by Jimmy Reese, the Padres were all interesting athletes. Baker himself was a former catcher, while Reese had been an infielder for the Oakland Oaks during the Roaring '20s.

Reese was easily my favorite on the team. With a cigar in his mouth, silver hair, and an engaging smile, it was a treat to watch him during infield practice. A former major leaguer and teammate of Babe Ruth, by the time he joined the Padres he was in his late forties or early fifties but still in remarkable physical condition. He was an expert with the fungo bat, a bat half the width of a regular bat and light enough to place the ball in any desired location . . . if you connect. He could place the ball anywhere. Among coaches, Reese was by far in a class by himself.

Padres' trainer Les Cook had been a catcher with the Hollywood Stars and the Sacramento Solons. He was in his early forties, loaded with energy and good at his job. He made it clear what he expected from the batboys. Once in a while, he called me over to tell me some risqué story. I always had time to listen; after all, it added to my store of knowledge. Les was good at his trade too, with very strong hands. He liked shaking our hands, if for no other reason than to test our strength.

Padres' pitcher "Toothpick Sam" Jones stood out. He had established a career in the Negro Leagues then Cleveland signed him and sent him to San Diego. At twenty-six, he was an imposing figure on the mound standing six-feet-four and weighing close to 200 pounds. He had a wicked curve ball coupled with an effective fast ball. He

Double trouble: Max West and Jack Graham

51

loved our ballpark and told me in the on-deck circle, "Lots of outfield with high fences."

Left-handed slugging outfielder Jack Graham was only one of a few players who hit a homerun over the right-field bleachers, a massive 400-foot drive. At thirty-five, this was his fourteenth season in baseball and his third year with the Padres. It was exciting to follow the ball when he connected. Bespectacled, it seemed like the extra pair of eyes worked for him. I got to know him more when he was traded to the Seals near mid-season. He had a reputation for hitting homeruns everywhere he played, but in the far reaches of Seals Stadium he had his work cut out for him. Most of the ballparks in the league had easy-to-reach outfield fences.

San Diego was followed by the Sacramento Solons who came to play a weekend series. The marquee proclaimed an 8:15 Friday night game. Most working people found time to attend weekend night and day games to their liking and attendance usually picked up. Sacramento wasn't the top attraction but their homebase was close enough to the Bay Area for fans to travel. The Solons had a new manager in Joe Gordon, former infielder and clutch hitter for the New York Yankees and the Cleveland Indians. This was Gordon's first year as manager. He succeeded Red Kress and Joe Marty whose managing had led the team into last place. Anything Joe did would be an improvement. He was someone to learn from since I thought of myself as a second baseman and shortstop. I kept my eyes glued on him when he took infield and batting practice as well as during the game.

I met Joe Marty for the first time during that series in the second week in May. I recognized him from the Signal Oil baseball cards and from games at Oaks Park. When the timing was right, I asked him what he liked about playing ball. He said breaking in with the Seals in 1934 and playing on the same team with Joe DiMaggio was something he would never forget. He said the area I was working near the on-deck circle was all dirt then. There were no bleachers in right or left field and you had to eat a hefty steak dinner to hit one over the fences. He played in a number of major league ballparks for about five years and felt that Seals Stadium was a major league ballpark in every way. At thirty-eight, he was near the end of his career, but he was kind enough to share his thoughts.

What a ballclub! The Solons had veterans with established careers like Joe Gordon and Joe Marty. They also had the future of the game in the person of first baseman Bob Boyd. Fresh from the Negro Leagues, now in his second year in organized baseball, Boyd was the consummate athlete. He was only twenty-five years old and destined for greatness. I made it a point to observe him in pre-game practice as well as during the game. He was not tall but was solidly built and ready to show the fans and opposing players his remarkable abilities. I couldn't help but stare as he took his warm-up swings. Bad news for the opposing pitchers! In addition to his fielding, he could hit with authority and steal bases along the way.

Sacramento was the last of the seven clubs to make their first visit to San Francisco during my first season. They all come back twice more before the season ended on September 9th. I found the visiting teams much more fascinating than their names in the box scores. Going on sixteen it was clear to me that baseball was an outdoor classroom with a lot to teach about the human condition. When the season ended, I was already immersing myself in my other learning environment at Berkeley High School.

7

Recovering Bats,
Chasing Fouls

In spite of my new confidence after a first year with the Seals, I found **life in high school perplexing.** The class schedule and the other sophomores who came from Garfield and Willard junior high schools both challenged me. I adjusted by acquiring new classmates. As a "shop boy," most of my classes were vocational or "industrial." Most kids from Berkeley's flat lands were similarly tracked; because we were from lower income working families the school district's adopted policy placed us in non-academic vocational courses. Therefore, we were relatively segregated from the kids who came from wealthier homes in the East Bay hills. Only in English class, did we mix with students assumed to be college-bound.

In physical education, the playing field was finally level between kids from both sides of the track. No matter what your family's background or income were, P.E. tested everyone in an even-handed way. Exercises and intramural sports sparked our testosterone no matter who we were or what part of town we had grown up in.

Off and on during the winter, I worked for Mrs. Troiel's small metal-fabricating shop across from where I lived. The job gave me some additional spending money. I found time enough to do my homework and adjust to the challenges of high school, although a budding high-school romance sidelined my efforts to try out for varsity baseball. Instead, I looked forward to the 1952 PCL season and applied myself to work, school, and love.

When spring training finally arrived, I returned to Seals Stadium for the first major league exhibition games. Manager O'Doul was gone. He had been replaced by Tommy Heath. Tommy was very different from O'Doul. For one thing, he had a vernacular well worth the price of admission to the ballpark. He spoke his mind with a dry sense of humor. For example, he referred to Doc Hughes as "the Healer," which prompted laughter from those close enough to hear. Tommy faced the challenge of having to bring the Seals up to a competitive level, for which he had to depend on coach Sprinz who acquainted him with PCL teams. The Seals were in last place.

Tommy Heath, manager

O'Doul had an international reputation, so replacing him must have been a formidable task. Tommy was direct and folksy, yet thoughtful. He had a sense of what was possible but in many ways he was quite ordinary. He was not particularly suave, in manner or dress, and was on the portly side of having a good physique. Still, his exterior did not determine his success; he turned out to have massive baseball savvy.

Tommy had managed the Minneapolis Millers of the American Association. When he came to San Francisco, he depended on the staff and his knowledge of ballplayers to assemble a competitive team. Over the winter, while I was working away at school, Tommy coordinated several trades that brought new faces to the Seals for spring training. President Fagan was determined to spend whatever it took to avoid landing in last place for a second year in a row. He had given Tommy a fairly free hand in picking new players.

To my delight, Jim Moran returned from the Oaks to take over second base. Once again, I was able to catch rides with him to Seals Stadium. Rookie catcher Will Tiesiera, a Castlemont High graduate from East Oakland, joined our commute. Will had spent the previous season at the Seals' farm club in Yakima, Washington, as part of the Western International League. Like Jim, Will was a good conversationalist. I learned a lot listening to these two men on our trips to and from the City.

Among the pitchers picked for the team, there was twenty-five year old left-hander Bill Boemler, and thirty-one year old right-hander Bill Bradford. Boemler stood six feet, six inches and could throw hard. He had worked as a stagehand for MGM Studios and his stories—particular the ones about attractive starlets—enthralled us. (I think he might have exaggerated some details for my benefit but I still listened eagerly.)

Bradford was also over six feet tall and considered himself a fun-loving Southern gentleman from Choctaw, Arkansas. During his fourth year in baseball, he demonstrated a variety of curve balls, fast balls, and change-ups. Bradford lived in the East Bay, so there were times I rode with him as well as with Moran.

The Seals' pitching staff also included returning veterans Elmer Singleton and Al Lien. Elmer, a smooth-throwing right-hander with plenty of good stuff on the mound, was in his fifteenth year playing ball at age thirty-four. He had come through several major league clubs as a class-act pitcher.

Bill Bevens joined the Seals mid-season. He was a big right-handed thirty-six year old player, a former New York Yankee. Bob Muncrief, another big right-handed pitcher, was also added to the team. He had at least twelve years experience in the big leagues.

We had another right-hander on the staff—Will Hafey—who was the former pitching sensation for the Oaks. At thirty-one and standing six-feet-two, he was well liked for many reasons, not least for his tremendous smile. He lived in Berkeley near Dwight Way and Telegraph Avenue—about two miles from my house. Without much prompting, he generously allowed me to tag along with him to and from the ballpark on a number of occasions. Often, he joined the batboys to play "over the line" before the team had to begin batting practice. Will was used in the outfield and as a hitter with authority.

The older pitchers relied on the younger catchers to guide them through the season. Ray Orteig performed for most of the season, with Nini Tornay and Will Tiesiera splitting the remainder of the games. I often wondered if these ex-major league pitchers allowed their young catchers to call all or most of the pitches. I never knew for sure but I suspected that Elmer Singleton, at least, made his own choice of pitches. In addition to being a skilled catcher, Tiesiera threw one of the most wicked knuckleballs I ever saw. It danced all over the place and made it impossible to catch. Near the end of the season, I surprised Tiesiera when a ball got loose in the bull pen. I nonchalantly picked it up and threw back a knuckler that floated all the way. The look on his face was priceless.

Infielder Reno Cheso came from Vancouver of the Western International League to nail down the third-base position. Veteran infielder Lennie Ratto (formerly with Sacramento) joined us as a shortstop, while Joe Grace returned for another season at first base. Lennie and Jim worked double-plays effectively, while Reno proved competitive with many outstanding ballplayers. Returning veteran Ray Hamrick was used at second or third base, or as shortstop.

Veteran players Bill McCawley and Bob Thurman returned for another season, joining newcomers Frankie Kalin, Gene Klinger, and Sal Taormina. Sal was not new to Seals fans—he had begun his baseball career in 1942 with the Seals, and then came back in 1946 after military service to help win the pennant. In 1947 and '48, he helped tie for it again. Strong as a bull, just under six-feet tall, Sal could play infield as well as outfield He had enjoyed a good year in Yakima in 1951 where he hit almost .300. That was what earned him the spot in San Francisco.

My cohorts, Buzzy and Bob, also returned as batboys although it would be their last season. Our assignments were the same as in the year before. We continued to work out with the ballclub during batting and infield practice. I don't know if this surprised Tommy, but he stayed in the dugout long enough to determine if we had any potential. When we trotted off the field, he shouted: "You guys would be out and out dangerous with some height!" Don Rode usually joined us when he completed his pre-game work. He pitched batting practice whenever the opportunity presented itself and threw the ball with uncanny accuracy.

Tommy's ability to compliment good performance extended to the groundskeepers. He seemed in awe of Seals Stadium and the work that it took to keep it in impeccable condition. Once, during his first season, he looked around, surveying the lush green outfield and manicured infield. "You guys have one helluva job maintaining this Taj Mahal," he said to Harvey and Shorty.

The 1952 Season Begins

The 1952 season saw the return of the seven-game series beginning on Tuesday, April 1st. The Seals opened—as they had the previous year—playing against the Portland Beavers. Clay Hopper, former manager of Montreal in the International League, replaced Bill Sweeney who had gone north to join the Seattle Rainiers. Clay was Jackie Robinson's first manager when Branch Rickey signed Robinson to a contract in 1946.

Among the returning regulars for the Beavers were Frankie Austin, Eddie Basinski, Joe Brovia, and Marino Pieretti. It was good to see them all again. When they came out of the dugout, onto the field, I welcomed each one back. I was not as shy as I had been the year before; still, I was not overly confident either. I showed the visiting players the respect and consideration they deserved. Marino went out of his way to put me at ease. We may have been *simpatico* because we were about the same size, or maybe it was our shared love for Mario Lanza and opera arias.

Among the newer faces playing for Portland were those of outfielder Granny Gladstone—a tall thin Panamanian totally new to the PCL after spending time in the Negro Leagues—and catcher Jim Gladd who had been a Seals team member in 1947.

When Portland left after a Sunday doubleheader, the Seals readied themselves for a weeklong series across the Bay. Since each of the eight PCL teams had batboys to work with the visiting teams, batboys did not travel with their teams when they went on the road. We could suit up and join the team if we could or wanted to, but we were not paid just to sit in the dugout during out-of-town games. When the Seals went on the road, I opted to spend my time developing a high-school romance instead.

The next team to come to San Francisco was the San Diego Padres who arrived at Seals Stadium on Tuesday night, April 15. Replacing their former manager Del Baker was none other than Frank O'Doul! You can't keep a good man down! The fans welcomed one of their favorite sons and O'Doul showed his pleasure in his loyal followers and the local press. He remembered me and reminded me to keep up with my school work. As I watched him with his new team, I gained a valuable lesson: Getting fired wasn't the end of the world. Instead, it provided an opportunity to change and command a new situation.

Two days later, Joe Gordon brought the Sacramento Solons to town for the Seals' first encounter with them in the new season. Joe returned with Joe Marty but brilliant Bob Boyd was missing from the roster. Taking his place at first base was left-handed batting sensation Bill Glynn—one of the nicest players I ever met. Bill had everything going for him; he was good with both glove and bat.

Two other players from Sacramento caught my eye: Richie Myers, a diminutive solid-hitting shortstop blessed with enormous talent, and Eddie Bockman, who had come from the Beavers to be a utility player. Eddie could hit consistently; on the third day, he demonstrated his skill at the plate.

Less than 1,000 people came out on Thursday night to witness one of the best pitched games that ever took place at Seals Stadium. The Solons' pitcher kept the Seals scoreless for twelve innings. On the Seals' side, right-handed pitcher Elmer Singleton carried a no-hitter against the Solons into the twelfth inning. Neither team had scored a run. With a runner on second base, Eddie Bockman came up and laced a line drive into left field, which put Sacramento on top as the game went into the bottom of the twelfth. Unfortunately, the Seals could not score a run and Elmer lost his bid for a no-hitter.

After the game, everybody came back into the clubhouse feeling bad for Elmer. Don Rode picked up a sandwich and a cold beer to offer the hard-luck pitcher. I don't remember whether or not Bob Stevens from the *Chronicle* came in for a story, or if manager Tom Heath said anything. I don't remember who drove me home that night,

Elmer Singleton, pitcher

whether it was Jim Moran, Bill Bradford, or Will Hafey. What I *do* remember from that night was Elmer's magnificent pitching performance.

Sacramento was a ballclub with little money. Whenever they came to San Francisco, they arrived with a bunch of talented players and good staff. Trainer Mike Chambers was a gentle fellow with a great physique; whenever the pitchers needed to stretch their muscles, they were in his qualified hands. He applied his strengthening touch to any player in need. On one visit to Seals Stadium, Richie Myers got the wind knocked out of him from either a hard slide into second base or a ball taking a bad hop that knocked him down. Mike ran out of the dugout to attend to the injured shortstop, reached down and scooped Richie up in his massive arms and carried him off the field.

When the Seals traveled south to Lane Field in San Diego, then on to Gilmore Field, the home of the Hollywood Stars, I had two weeks off. By the end of the first week, I received my second semester report card from Berkeley High School: three C's, a B, and one A. Mr. Marker noted that there was "too much yapping" in my Industrial Drawing class. The pressure was to bring my grades up in English IV, Industrial Drawing, and my Vocational Print Shop classes. The final semester reports would come out on Friday, June 13. I was sixteen going on seventeen, and had been making the most out of my social life. For the brief times when I was off-duty with the Seals, I knew I had to focus on school.

On May 13, Bill Sweeney brought his Seattle Rainiers to San Francisco. They were a battling ballclub destined for placement in the first division. Sweeney had replaced the great Rogers Hornsby as manager. The league's leading hitter, Jim Rivera, was also gone and on his way to the big leagues. Marv Grissom, a twenty game winner, had moved up to pitch for the Chicago White Sox. Infielder Artie Wilson joined Seattle after a stint with the 1951 New York Giants. As Sweeney's starting shortstop, Artie still made aggressive good plays. First baseman Bob Boyd returned to Seattle after a few games with the Chicago White Sox, bringing his consistent hitting skills to the Rainiers. Like Artie, Bob Boyd could do it all: run, hit, and field. He had major league written all over him.

Seattle had retained right-handed pitcher Vern Kindsfather who had spent part of the previous season with Memphis (the American Association). At age twenty-six, Kindsfather had an assortment of pitches to work to his advantage. One-and-a-half months into the season, he and right-handed Al Widmar were like cats toying with mice as they dazzled the hitters.

The Seals spent the next week trying to regain their dignity doing battle against Clay Hopper's Lucky Beavers at Vaughn Street Park in Portland. I used the time to revive my grades and reconnect with my West Berkeley pals. Of course, I preferred playing with them to hitting the books, but I tried hard to complete school assignments.

On May 27, the Los Angeles Angels made their first trip of 1952 to San Francisco. I looked forward to seeing these players again; as a club, they were especially pleasant for me to work with. When the Angels took batting practice, I visited with trainer Dave Flores. He wanted a rundown on my school activities and let me know that he thought it was important to get a good education. But, he also acknowledged how hard it must be when distracted by virtuous teenage girls. The blush on my face told him that sometimes I yielded to such distractions.

Back on the field, I noticed returning shortstop Gene Baker. Both he and second baseman Jackie Hollis worked double-plays to perfection during both infield practice and the nine subsequent innings. Chuck Connors also played for the Angels that season; he was already a popular actor and a favorite with all the fans. Nevertheless, Ron Northey was the player who stood out for me as one of the strongest and most agile on the field. Max West was far less muscular but had excellent eye-to-hand coordination and was a consistent left-handed slugger. Since starting in 1935, Max was in his eighth PCL season. He was an attraction in the batting cage as he lined shots into right field. The former major leaguer was almost thirty-seven years of age but he still had a lot of fire power in his swing.

Manager Stan Hack had put together another skillful ballclub for the Angels. Only two months into the season, they were playing like they had a chance at the pennant. Oakland, Hollywood, San Diego, and Seattle came out of that year's starting gate with the flag in mind as well. Sacramento and the Seals had their work cut out if they wanted to get into the first division. The Angels left town after Sunday's games. The Seals headed north to Seattle.

Fred Haney brought his Hollywood Stars for a week of games beginning Tuesday night, June 10th. The marquee advertised their arrival and the newspapers heralded the series; some good-sized crowds turned out for a number of reasons. The Hollywood team was on top of the standings and their new outfielder, Carlos Bernier, was having an incredible season.

Carlos Bernier carried 180 pounds on a five-foot-eight inch frame and was pure dynamite with tightly packed muscles and amazing speed. He played with tremendous intensity. When he took practice swings in the on-deck circle that Tuesday evening, he looked over at me and asked my name. I told him. Then he asked if I spoke Spanish. I told him I didn't. He shook my hand and said, "Mucho gusto." I liked him right away.

Carlos Bernier, outfielder

After the game, I returned the bats to the Visitors Clubhouse and was stopped by trainer Frankie Jacobs who asked, "Who's it gonna be, Carlos or me?" I was caught off guard and didn't know what to say, so I said nothing and continued putting the bats in the rack. He grabbed me and said he would take care of me. I made no eye contact but scampered out as fast as my chubby legs could take me. On the way back to the Seals Clubhouse, I remembered what Memo Luna had told me and what Frankie Jacobs said the first time I met him: "Wanna go a couple of rounds?'

Before the end of the week, Carlos and I had another interaction. It happened during a day game with a crowd of people there to witness the whole thing. Carlos had struck out. As he walked away from the batter's box, bat in hand, he turned and looked right at me. I was standing some twenty feet away. Then, suddenly, he threw the bat towards me with such force that the bat hit the grass then somersaulted into my hand. I caught it. It must have looked planned, but it was not. I looked at Carlos and saw that he was relieved that I didn't get hurt. After that, we became good friends but there was always a sense that we were tolerating one another.

The Hollywood Stars had a running ballclub that included outfielders Tommy Saffell and Ted Beard. Fred Haney also had a productive pitching staff with Mel Queen, Johnny Lindell, Paul Pettit, and Jim Walsh. Because they had an agreement with the Pittsburgh Pirates, the Stars were able to acquire fine ballplayers.

Before Will Hafey picked me up on Friday the 13th, my mother showed me the envelope containing my report card that had just arrived in the mail. She had a serious look on her face as I opened it. Three B's, a C, and one A. Mr. Marker had given me the one C for Industrial Drawing. Relieved, I was in good spirits as Will and I headed toward San Francisco that night, though when we arrived Buzzy and Bob were not there. Because they had graduated from their high schools, their work with the Seals had come to an end. Don Rode broke the news. When the Seals came back from Sacramento, I would take over the ballboy job and wear the pin-stripes of the Seals uniform. He hired two new batboys during the week.

New Hands on Deck

Before the June 24th game, Don introduced me to Frank Donofrio and Bobby Ferguson, the two new batboys. Bobby was a blue-eyed blond boy; he was given the number 77 Seals uniform. Frankie was dark-haired and brown-eyed and was given the Visitors uniform 00. I inherited the 88 white pin-striped home team uniform. I took my new compatriots down to the field and we shagged fly balls during batting practice. Afterwards, I went up to the umpire's dressing room, introduced myself and carried the box that contained the three-dozen balls for the game back down to the field. Gordon Ford, Al Summers, and Joe Iaocovetti recognized me from my work with the visiting clubs.

The Oaks were taking infield practice when I appeared from the Seals dugout prior to the game. Three months into the season and Oakland had another top-notch ballclub. Bay Area fans came out to witness this series and to keep the rivalry alive. There had been few changes from last year's club and I enjoyed saying hello to the guys I recognized. Johnny Jorgensen congratulated me on my promotion and reminded me "not to get too big for my britches." Piper Davis came back to lead the club in hitting. Cowboy pitcher Allen Gettel returned and was also having a good year.

First baseman Tookie Gilbert and utility infielder Hank Schenz were new to the club. Outfielder and former Philadelphia Athletic Sam Chapman had returned to his Bay Area roots. He was over thirty-six years old but could still hit that long ball. Somewhat younger but also with an effective batting technique, Pete Milne came to town prepared to do some damage. The Oaks had picked up catcher Rafael Noble from the New York Giants. Rafael was from Central Hatillo, Cuba; he was something to watch in the batting cage as he took swings.

My new assignment as the ballboy meant that I would work next to the Seals on the third-base side of the backstop, opposite from where I had been situated as the Visitors' batboy. This new position gave me a clear view of both foul lines. My job was to retrieve all foul balls on the field and return them to the home plate umpire for his inspection and use. At this time, the job of chasing balls was solely that of the ballboy with occasional help from the bull pen. I had watched track-star Bobby Rodriguez do it the previous year, as he flew down the foul lines in hot pursuit of the ball. On plush grass—often damp on summer nights in San Francisco—you could hear me whizzing past the dugouts on my way down the lines. In Seals Stadium, that was going a long way, 365 feet from home plate on the left field and 350 feet on the right field. If there were any players from the bull pens on the field, they might save me a few steps. However, my endurance was regularly tested by players who consistently hit foul balls.

I worked with all of the umpires and learned to appreciate their role in the game and how seemingly thankless their jobs were. They had to make split-second decisions and took their responsibility seriously. From these dedicated men, I learned a lot about tenacity and courage. Most umpires had the respect and admiration of the players, but once in awhile you could hear screaming from the dugout if a questionable call was made.

During the first year in my new job, I learned more about baseball than ever. The strike zone was a clear area located above the batter's knees to below his shoulders, directly over the plate. Lightning fast action, the noise of the crowd, and the sound of the bat missing a ball caught by the catcher all kept me on my toes; responding to these cues, while not getting distracted took good eyes and a strong heart.

During my second season with the Seals, I was able to get to know many umpires: Bill Anske, Roman Bentz, Cece Carlucci, Gordon Ford, Joe Iaocovetti,

Al Mutart, Chris Pelakoudas, Jack "King" Powell, film actor Gil Stratton and Al Summers. My favorite ones had a sense of humor combined with a strong discipline about how the game was played, both qualities that were essential for defusing a heated call.

The Oaks came to the City in 1952 and when they left they were near the top of the standings. Manager Mel Ott and owner Brick Laws had simply put together an outstanding ballclub. Before the Oaks left town, I had the chance to befriend Johnny Jorgensen and get a new life lesson. The "Spider" shared information calculated to make me a better ballplayer. He told me that "it was not the size of the glove but how a player used it." I looked down at my glove—a large one given to me by rookie pitcher Ernie Domenichelli. I looked over at Spider's; it looked like something from a kid's toy store.

After a week in Los Angeles battling our southland rivals, the Seals returned for a final homestand with Joe Gordon's Sacramento club. Tommy Heath and Joe Gordon tried everything to avoid being left on the bottom. Sacramento had sent us there in '51, and by the middle of July 1952, we were battling it out again with them, trying to reach the first division. It made for good baseball even if the fans didn't bust down the turnstile to watch the struggle. Pitchers Glen Elliott and Jess Flores gave us fits while Bill Glynn and Richie Myers banged the ball all over the place. I kept myself in shape trying to stay on top of the balls hit on the far side of the chalk lines.

After the Solons left town, both teams were still almost intact. The Seals had to face Oakland for a weeklong series on their turf. Although I was on vacation, I suited up and worked out with the Seals anyway. I saw Howard Storm, the Oaks' batboy. I had played basketball with him at the West Berkeley YMCA when we were both in grammar school. Howard's team was now in first place and my team was floundering near the cellar. Although a lot of homeruns were hit that week, it was the Oaks doing the running around the bases. Meanwhile, the Hollywood Stars were hoping that the Seals would rise to the occasion and clobber the Oaks so that they could take over first place.

Sunday's doubleheader turned out a good crowd. Everybody in the stands was enjoying their team's first-place perch. With each pitch, the Oaks responded with something meaningful. Then, it happened. I have heard about ballplayers brawling but I had never seen anything come close to a fight during my two seasons in the PCL. Boemler got the call from Tommy to start the first game. Left-handed, he had a big job trying to strike out the Oaks top hitters, Rafael Noble and Piper Davis.

I don't remember which inning it was, maybe the fourth. It happened so fast. Piper Davis was hitting. After a couple of pitches, Boemler knocked him down with an inside pitch. The Seals' pitchers had been throwing at him for the better part of the weeklong series. Piper slams the next pitch for a single. Right-handed hitter Johnny Ostrowski bunts down the third-base side as Reno Cheso picks it up and throws it along the ground to first. Joe Grace comes up with the ball, but throws it past Jim Moran, who runs down the ball and throws it past third. Piper Davis had run on the bunt, and was still running as the ball traveled all over the infield. Rounding third base, and heading for home, Davis and the ball thrown by Moran to Boemler at home plate arrived one after the other. Boemler was ready to make the tag when Davis slid upward and knocked Boemler to the ground. Both dugouts quickly emptied out onto the field and we were in the middle of a donnybrook.

The fans of both teams were screaming at their players to get in the best blows. Maybe it was the usherettes, but somebody alerted the Emeryville Police Department to restore order. I was in the dugout until it happened and had jumped out only to get a closer look. From his spot at home plate, Howard Storm motioned to me to join the fracas. I hoped he was kidding. I'm not a fighter but he was, and the fact that he was two inches shorter than me only meant he was twice as mean.

I turned on my Mexican charm and smiled at him. Meanwhile the fists were flying everywhere. Both managers took one on the gourd. Noble was throwing right hands at anything alive while Sal Taormina grabbed him from behind and wrestled him to the ground. Photographers for the wire services and the Oakland newspapers were snapping shots while trying to avoid getting hit.

Howard and I stared at one another, while my smile slowly evaporated and fear overtook me. After fifteen or twenty minutes, peace was finally restored. The home plate umpire assessed the damage and called the game back to order.

I don't know who won the fight but the Seals won both games of the doubleheader, knocking the Oaks out of first place. The next day, the Bay Area's newspapers featured many stories: some of them even got a few facts right.

With only a month and a half left in the season, Tommy and his brigade still had to tangle with the seven other clubs one more time both at home and away. I spent the remainder of the summer when the Seals were on the road with the guys from my neighborhood. We played softball, basketball, and touch football on the Columbus School playground, the closest park to our homes. Some of us took in a movie uptown in Berkeley at United Artists or the California theaters. I had some money in my wallet which I used to buy clothes for school. Near the end of the season, we received special leather wallets made by an out-of-state prison inmate who had most of the PCL teams ordering from him. The wallets were genuine leather, double-stitched with our names notched on one side and the name of the ballclub on the other side.

Tommy raised the Seals standing by one notch. He taught me that there was dignity in anything as long as we stayed the course. We closed out that home season with a September 14 doubleheader against the Los Angeles Angels. They would finish nine games ahead of us to capture sixth place. With one week left, the Seals traveled north to a four-game series with Seattle and a final four-game series with Portland. Even if we lost all eight games, we would not end up in the cellar two years in a row. I followed the team on Don Klein's radio broadcasts.

After that last game, Will Hafey and I returned to Berkeley. I started the fall semester of my junior year in high school the following Monday. As my second year with the Seals came to an end, I realized that I had not noticed the decline in attendance.

8

Flying Down
the Foul Lines

One month after the 1952 baseball season, I received my mid-semester grades: two A's, two B's, and a C. Miss Mary Banks, my English teacher correctly recorded my habit of disturbing fellow classmates. The low grade was meant to catch my attention: it did. I returned to her classroom the next semester with a more cooperative attitude. My A's were in Vocational Printing (due to Mr. Austin M. Waltz, a new instructor) and P.E. In his class, my efforts to improve my concentration had succeeded. By the end of the first semester, most of my grades rose while one sank nearly to the bottom: I received 4A's and a D—I almost had reason to celebrate.

I worked for five different employers in 1953, trying to balance school with my blossoming social life. Teachers Walter Miller and Ray Hernandez of the Vocational Education Department had helped me get jobs at both the Berkeley Public Library and at Green Printing Company, a small shop in Emeryville. I also continued my part-time job at Mrs. Troiel's metal fabricating shop.

By early March it was time for tryouts on the high school's varsity baseball team. I was one of four candidates by mid-March for the second-base position but coach George Wilson selected four-letter man Carletus Gordon to fill the spot; he was right to do so. Even though I was disappointed, I recognized Carletus' abilities.

Then, it was time again for the Seals to begin their traditional two-week schedule of exhibition games. It was like coming back home when I returned to Seals Stadium to resume my duties as ballboy. Don Rode had promoted Frankie Donofrio into the Visitors Clubhouse and hired Johnny McCormack as the Visitors' batboy. Bob Ferguson came back as the Seals' batboy. My duties as ballboy continued.

Manager Tommy Heath and the front office had made several changes to the Seals line-up in an effort to rise to the first division. Long-time coach Joe Sprinz was promoted to Chief Scout; his former role was filled by Harlan Clift, Tommy's one-time teammate. In the late 1930s, Harlan was a hard-hitting third-baseman for the St. Louis Browns and the Washington Senators of the American League. During pre-game infield practice sessions, he worked with the batboys to entertain the fans.

The '53 Seals included several returning players and some new ones who arrived as a result of acquisitions, trades, or the farm system. Seattle first baseman George Vico replaced Joe Grace at first base. Leo Righetti replaced Lennie Ratto at shortstop, returning to the PCL from Charleston of the American Association. Jim Moran returned for his fifth season to anchor the second-base position, while Reno Cheso once again covered the hot corner.

Leo Righetti, shortstop

Bill McCawley and Sal Taormina returned for another season in outfield. Rookie outfielder Jerry Zuvela from San Pedro, California, joined us after three years in Yakima. Long-ball hitter, outfielder-pitcher Al Lyons arrived as a result of a trade with Seattle and we picked up another long-ball hitter and outfielder—Frankie Kalin—in a trade with the American Association's Indianapolis team. Seals' catcher Ray Orteig was traded to Seattle; that left Nini Tornay and Will Tiesiera behind-the-plate.

Six pitchers returned: Bill Boemler, Bill Bradford, Al Lien, Bob Muncrief, Elmer Singleton, and Walter Clough. Southpaw Windy McCall came over from Birmingham (American Association), and right-hander Ted Shandor arrived from Yakima. Over the next six months, Tommy Heath would discover whether or not his second season in the league would be an improvement over his seventh-place finish the previous year. He was banking on this new line-up of players.

My third season with the club kept me in shape running after foul balls. Like Bobby Rodriguez before me, I became the unofficial leader of the batboys. I spent time in the clubhouse before each game helping Don in whatever way I could. Although I did not give orders to the other batboys, I learned that seniority had its rewards. I could spin many tales about what it was like before the new batboys had joined the Seals. I often urged Johnny and Bobby to glimpse into the box seats at the marvelous silhouettes of the usherettes as they sashayed up and down the aisles; they appreciated my helpful hints.

Chasing down foul balls meant having less contact with the visiting players, many of whom I had become acquainted with during my first two years. The foul balls that were hit down the first-base side into right field brought me into contact with the opposition's bull pen and some familiar faces and although I used every opportunity to greet the players, my "hello" often trailed in the wind as I chased the ball. "Here comes running Bill, never was and never will," one of them joked. It wasn't easy running and laughing back to home plate.

On Tuesday night, April 7, Los Angeles Angels' manager Stan Hack brought an outstanding ballclub into San Francisco. When the team emerged from the dugout for batting and infield practice, I had a chance to renew my friendships with trainer Dave Flores and some of the returning regulars: Gene Baker, Chuck Connors, Calvin McLish, and Max West all remembered me from when I was their batboy and wearing '00.' The best I could do was wave or yell to catch their attention as I did my job. McLish told me to slow down as I whizzed by their bull pen when a ball was hit foul on the other side of the field. The visiting players I once had worked for seemed to enjoy seeing me in my new assignment.

The Seals spent two weeks on the road, first to Oakland then Los Angeles. One of my favorite managers, Bill Sweeney, arrived at Seals Stadium with his high-flying Seattle ballclub for a weeklong series that began on April 28. I looked forward to seeing Artie Wilson again, as well as several ex-Seals including catcher Ray Orteig and outfielder Jackie Tobin. When Jackie reminded me to pace myself running after foul balls, I tried to follow his advice. With a grin on his face, Ray told me to watch out for gopher holes near the left-field corner. I never did see anything that resembled a hole out there.

Sweeney knew how to get the best from his players. I took stock of their shortstop remembering he had played for the Oaks. Merrill Combs was good with the glove. I noticed how he got rid of the ball making double plays and I copied his side-arm throw towards first base whenever I had an opportunity. I wanted to prepare myself in the event the shortstop position opened up at Berkeley High.

The Seals had their hands full trying to beat Seattle who was strong early in the season. They continued to get good pitching from Al Widmar and Vern Kindsfather, but my favorite among the pitchers was former Seals ace Steve Nagy. He had a couple of good seasons with San Francisco before I joined the ballclub. The left-handed pitcher, short in stature, looked like he was on his way to another good season backed by a pace-setting ballclub. Only four weeks into the season, Seattle came out of the gate looking like they could take the pennant.

Artie Wilson, shortstop

The Seals went south to Gilmore field to take on another red-hot team, the Hollywood Stars, and then returned for our first home series with Clay Hopper's Portland Beavers. Ex-Seals Dino Restelli and catcher Jim Gladd came with them. Frankie Austin, a steady-hitter and shortstop returned with reliable Eddie Basinski at second base and Hank Arft on first. Missing from the outfield was Joe Brovia who had been traded to Sacramento. In the early weeks of the season, Portland was getting solid pitching from Royce Lint who was having his second season with Portland after working with the Holly-wood Stars. To me, the Seals and Portland seemed evenly matched.

The Oakland Oaks arrived at Seals Stadium for a week-long series, Tuesday, May 25. Manager Galan brought in another solid ballclub including a new first baseman, Jim Marshall, one helluva hitter and all-around nice guy. Another personal favorite was Johnny Jorgensen who seemed quite pleased to watch me chase foul balls, telling me it was good for my legs. The Oaks had 'Two-Gun' Allen Gettel and George Bamberger, both awfully good pitchers. Ex-Seal Con Dempsey came back to baseball for his last year to help the club, and the Oaks also had a little left-hander with dazzling stuff who had attended Acalanes High in Contra Costa County: Don Ferrarese.

Overall I thought the Oaks had a solid ballclub with Piper Davis returning along with outfielder Pete Milne. The next several months tested their abilities against Seattle, Hollywood, and Los Angeles. The Bay Bridge rivalry was alive and kicking; it brought out a few more loyalists from both sides of the Bay. The Seals held their own . . . for a while but the Oaks had the better team. The Seals left town after the Sunday doubleheader and went north to Vaughn Street Park to face Portland.

Just as my last semester report card was due to arrive, the high-flying Hollywood Stars came to Seals Stadium. We had a good crowd and many newspaper writers wanting to get their first glimpse of the new manager Bobby Bragan and his gang of quality ballplayers. Now eleven weeks into the season, the Stars dominated the standings.

Trainer Frankie Jacobs stuck his head out of the dugout to yell "Show some hustle" as I raced down the first base foul line. I could only wave hello because the home plate umpire, Cece Carlucci, needed a fresh supply of baseballs. Carlucci and I worked well together; I appreciated his remarkable patience. Hollywood was a likable ballclub with first baseman Chuck Stevens; big Jack Phillips, the all-around infielder; and little Ted Beard, the speedy outfielder with the strong bat. I remembered them all from my time as Visitors' batboy.

Loaded with talent, the '53 Stars could consistently hit, run, and field. Bragan had them running a lot when they were on the bases, especially Tommy Saffell and Ted Beard. Right-handers George O'Donell and Jim Walsh led a strong pitching staff, yet it was the team's overall confidence that impressed me. I don't know what would have happened if Carlos Bernier had been on this team. (Saffell and Beard stole a total of 50 bases as compared to the 65 bases that Bernier had stolen the previous year). Bernier was spending his year in the outfield with the Pittsburgh Pirates who—as the parent club—were sending and receiving outstanding ballplayers to and from the Stars. This could translate into another pennant at Gilmore Field.

After the series with the Stars, which ended with them on top, the Seals traveled south to Lane Field and Lefty O'Doul's San Diego Padres. I followed the team on the radio as I began my first week of summer vacation. It was the best of summers for me, playing American Legion ball at San Pablo Park in South Berkeley with guys from the Berkeley High varsity team, including first baseman Earl Robinson; right-handed pitchers Rocci Giordano and Louie Gorham; and third baseman Eddie Kelly. We played against some of the finest Legion ballclubs in the East Bay, including players from Oakland's McClymonds and Technical high schools.

After their time in San Diego, the Seals returned to face manager Gene Desautels and his Sacramento ballclub for a seven-game series beginning Tuesday night, June 23. Outfielder Joe Brovia—traded from Portland—heaped serious damage on Paul Fagan's ballclub. Along with little Richie Myers, the big bats of outfielder Bob Dillinger and first baseman Nippy Jones, this was a competitive team. Joe was having another good year with his loud-talking bat. My good buddy, pitcher Chick Pieretti, came over with Brovia from Portland and he and I picked up were we left off, engaging in small talk near the bull pen. Crafty and sometimes daffy Chet Johnson returned for another season along with Kenny Gables and Bud Watkins. This had been a hard luck ballclub unable to capitalize on all their talents and lacking the money to strengthen some of their weaker areas.

From my position working with the umpires and running after foul balls, I saw the overall efforts of each ballclub and remained relatively uninterested in the teams' standings. I don't even recall picking up a newspaper to find out about the pennant races. Instead, I enjoyed seeing the men I knew from my first two seasons and renewing friendships. I enjoyed each player that I worked with, irregardless of the kind of season they were having. I played a lot of ball that summer but didn't fuss about my own batting average; instead, it was a sheer pleasure when I did make contact with the ball once in a while. I was growing up and enjoying myself in the process.

Before I could get too self-satisfied though, Lefty O'Doul brought his San Diego ballclub into his old haunts on Tuesday, June 30. I was surprised that he remembered me as he stopped me in my tracks to ask how I was doing.

He was talking to fans in the first row on the first-base side. I told him I was okay and he said he wasn't surprised because he expected big things from me. I wasn't used to this kind of attention and felt myself turning a few shades of red. Trainer Les Cook reached out and shook my hand, telling me to pay attention to the umpires and stop gawking at the girls in the stands. Jimmie Reese jumped in and told them to leave the kid alone. Somehow I survived the compliments and began to relax.

San Diego came to town with a pretty good ballclub and one of the hardest working guys, shortstop Buddy Peterson, on their team. Peterson played the game with great intensity and did almost anything to win. Outfielder Earl Rapp returned for another season, hitting singles, doubles, a few triples and a decent number of homeruns. My old nemesis Memo Luna returned and watched me run down the foul line near the bull pen. Instead of getting on me for not knowing Spanish, he just whistled and shook his hand at me. I knew he liked to tease me and that made me feel good. It was also good to see Lloyd Dickey, the left-handed pitcher again. O'Doul used the ex-Seal whenever he wanted to get the right-handed hitters out.

San Francisco spent the next two weeks traveling to Sacramento, San Diego, Seattle, and Portland. They returned to Seals Stadium on July 21 to begin another round of home games before season finale on September 13. In August, we picked up thirty-two year old Tony Ponce, a right-handed pitcher from Ventura of the Single A California League. I had never seen Ponce perform and it was a treat to watch him frustrate the big guys in the PCL. With whatever time left in the season, he won eight games in a row, including both games of the closing doubleheader against the Los Angeles Angels. Ponce possessed an array of fast balls, curves, slid-

Tony Ponce, pitcher

ers, and his own floating knuckle ball. (In my demented state of mind, I felt that the three best knuckle-ball pitchers in town were Tony, Will Tiesiera, and me!) Ponce was refreshingly different, a precursor of the future of baseball in America with an influx of passionate Latin American ballplayers.

Tommy Heath was able to raise the Seals to fifth place. Things seemed to be looking up. That's when President Paul Fagan decided to quit baseball, in part because the PCL failed to achieve major league status. Crowds had dwindled from the previous year, down by 25,000 from the previous seasons. Fagan was losing money. Less than a month after the season ended, Fagan handed the organization over to the man who had hired me, Damon Miller. It took several months to secure approval from the PCL's directors; Miller would first have to guarantee the team's solvency.

Meanwhile, I forged on with my high school education concerned about whatever future I might have with the Seals. Life would prove eventful over the next several months. Two months away from my eighteenth birthday, I was becoming increasingly aware of possible military obligations I might have. My future was unknown.

9

Life at Berkeley High

As the Seals opened their 1953 home schedule, it was an extremely **busy time for me.** I tried to keep up with games at high school and at Seals Stadium.

At last I made it into the lineup at Berkeley High, playing behind Carletus Gordon against Alameda High School. We never got the hits for starting pitcher Rocci Giordano and Alameda beat us 4-2. If that wasn't bad enough, I wasn't able to make it to the Block B dance that Friday night because of my job; the Seals had a night game against Seattle. It was starting to dawn on me that I had taken on too much. And, once again, report cards were about to come out.

My mother picked up the mail the week the Seals were playing in Sacramento. The look on her face told me everything: I had one A (in Vocational Printing), 2 Bs in English and Physical Education, a C in Industrial Science, and a D in U.S. History. My grades were showing signs of my inattention. Since I had stopped going to mass on Sundays, I was starting to think that it might be time to visit the confessional. I kept remembering the sign behind Leo Hughes' rubbing table and "kept trying."

I used my leisure time hanging out with the guys from West Berkeley, frequenting the YMCA, playing baseball at San Pablo and Kenney Parks and going to the movies. They were an important part of my life along with the record collection I began. I earned enough money at all of my part-time jobs to spend it as only a high school student could. I also took in some of the Berkeley High School functions: the Varieties, the Senior Play, and whatever was featured in the Community Theater. We'd get big names coming to Berkeley to perform, including Victor Borge and the Broadway production of *Guys and Dolls*.

I couldn't get enough of the movies. Whatever was playing uptown at the Berkeley, the California, or the United Artists' theaters I would take full advantage of on nights when I wasn't working. I liked everything including the MGM musicals: *Showboat, Singing in the Rain,* and *Kiss Me Kate.* I also liked good westerns like Gregory Peck in *The Gunfighter,* Gary Cooper in *High Noon,* and Alan Ladd in *Shane.* When Marlon Brando appeared in *The Men,* I began to see a different style of acting and that I enjoyed.

When Berkeley High took on the Richmond Oilers, we got knocked around badly. I got the starting assignment and reached base once in my usual non-threatening manner—with a walk. Richmond hit everything we tossed at them and trounced us 14-5. Then it happened. The next day, the Alameda Hornets came to Berkeley High's Biedenbach Field and I finally connected

Berkeley High's Biedenback Field

with something other than a base on balls. The ball sailed into right-center field one hop to the Girls' Gymnasium. It was my first opportunity to circle the bases on the way to home plate. The relay thrown from outfield to infield to catcher sent me back to third with a triple. Not to be undone the next time up, I bunted safely towards the second baseman for my second hit in one game. My contribution helped give us a 4-3 victory over the Hornets. Maybe I'm on my way.

To swing at a hard pitch and make solid contact with the bat was an exhilarating sensation. Up until that point, I had not had this experience in varsity baseball. At our next game—against San Lorenzo—I got another hit even though it did not help the final score of 6-4. What I felt was new, a once elusive feeling that was now becoming an expectation. Each time that I came up to the bat now, I was filled with an indescribable buoyancy. Unfortunately, this feeling was frequently thwarted by effective pitchers.

Against Castlemont, I walked in my only time at bat. Our coach sent his best nine players against McClymonds but we watched them knock the ball everywhere, beating Berkeley 9-3. McClymonds had good ballplayers in their lineup including Curt Flood, Frank Robinson, and Charlie Beamon. All three—and catcher Jesse Gonder—went on to promising careers. Both of Oakland's teams beat us decisively 9-3 and 4-1. When BHS played against Richmond High and won 5-3, I had mostly watched from the bench.

By May, when the Seals went against the Portland Beavers, Berkeley High traveled to El Cerrito to take on the Gauchos whose big right-handed pitcher, Ernie Broglio, was raised near San Pablo Park, not far from where I grew up. Broglio possessed a mean fast ball and a dazzling curve ball. I'm sure it was his curve ball that arched towards home plate that I hit—a solid blow over the shortstop's head for a single. I thought I was in my groove until little left-handed Grover Blackshear replaced Broglio. He had the deadliest of sinker balls as he set us down. Before the dust settled we were still able to beat them 8-3 behind the solid pitching of Manny Garcia.

I began to think that maybe the Seals and I would start producing in our respective environments. As the Seals headed to Seattle, BHS played its final game of the '53 ACAL season, beating Hayward High behind the good pitching of right-handed Ron Lundgren 3-0. I ended the season with another single and even scored a run. We came in fourth place as Richmond won the title. Richmond outfielder Don Moitoza was signed by the Oaks and sent to one of their farm clubs. El Cerrito's Ernie Broglio ended up pitching eleven games with the Oaks.

My social life was probably typical for teenagers in the early 1950s. My classmates were vague about their adventures with the opposite sex, so I could only speculate about the romantic adventures of my fellow students. My hormones were raging and my face was breaking out. After my mother's tried and true homemade remedies failed me, I checked with Henry Messina, owner of Henry's Drugs, who suggested Physicians and Surgeons brand soap. My fine Yardley hair and skin products with their distinctive British aromas were replaced by a plain medicinal brand—fragrance-free and dull to my teenage mind. It seemed like an affront to my sophisticated sensibilities.

I thought I was pretty suave in my Levi's with the turned-over and stitched cuffs and my faded blue or tan Peggers that I had bought myself at the House of Harris or Smith's in downtown Berkeley. My low-cut black leather shoes were always shined with a good paste wax and I wore them with brightly colored argyle socks. With a few bucks in my custom-made leather wallet, I was feeling pretty good . . . at least until the high-flying Hollywood Stars came north to challenge the Seals. This happened at just about the same time as my final report card arrived in West Berkeley.

I was about to find out if I had made it through my junior year. I got to the mailbox just a few steps ahead of my mother and picked up my final grades: 3 B's, 2 C's, and a D in U.S. History. The poorest grade was from Miss Beverly Barsamian, a dangerously attractive woman who had unfortunately correctly assessed my performance. I had started out with a C minus and ended with the D. My mother's demeanor showed that she had expected something better from me.

When our school year book, the *Olla Podrida*, arrived, I took it to Seals Stadium where shortstop Leo Righetti saw me lingering through the pages. He asked if he could look at it, then returned it with the following message: "To Billy, I will my bat so he can be a better hitter. Leo Righetti." I think it was meant to cheer me up.

As I faced the last months of my high school career, I reported to Biedenbach Field for coach Wilson's "spring training" in early March 1954. Mr. Wilson called upon his professional experiences to run us through the maneuvers we needed to compete in the ACAL. He showed us how to bunt with the front-end of the bat pointed at the pitcher, executing it to perfection. He ran us through several offensive plays with runners on first and third and taught us the signals for executing his directions. He taught us the basics of the game which would prove useful after graduation on whatever diamonds we faced. I got the starting assignment at shortstop as the pre-season games began.

By mid-March we were scheduled to play the University of California Freshmen on our home field and then the rains came. On Friday, March 12 we beat Oakland High 7-3. I had a good day, good for me, going 0 for 1. For a leadoff hitter I've got to do better. The following Tuesday we lost to Castlemont 2-0; I had walked a couple of times. Two days later I got my second hit

My Berkeley High baseball team: Back row, left to right: Jerry Christie, Lance Renner, Lloyd Penn, Buddy Bozonier, Bennie Walker, Earl Robinson, Eddie Kelly, Rocci Giordano, Bob Van Heuit. Front row, left to right: Jack Hooper, Levi Domenic, Billy Soto

of the season against the Cal Frosh which contributed to our narrow victory of 3-2. That Friday night, the Seals opened their two-weeks of major league exhibition games against the Pittsburgh Pirates. It was my first day back to work and it was good to be back.

Berkeley High continued its season on March 29 against the Fremont High Tigers. Right-handed pitcher Louie Gorham didn't get the full force of our offensive punch; I go 1 for 3 while we lose 4-3. We don't feel too good about it but coach Wilson tells us 'not to keep our daubers down.' I think that's what he said. I tended to hear what I wanted to hear. The ACAL season opened the following week. I hit safely in two games but with our team losing, it didn't make me feel any better. Even with fifteen hits in two games it wasn't enough for pitchers Manny Garcia and Rocci Giordano. Coach Wilson doesn't lose his temper but tells us to concentrate on the basics.

Coach Wilson kept us on target with practice sessions. Several were scheduled during the week that the Hollywood Stars came to Seals Stadium and I missed Wednesday's practice because of my clubhouse duties. Coach Wilson called me into his office to discuss my absence. He tells me that it's not fair to the rest of the guys. I don't have much of an excuse other than to say I get some infield practice at Seals Stadium. He listened, then told me that I was off the team. What could I say? I shrugged my shoulders, shook his hand, and told him I appreciated his help and that I would put it to good use. Then, I vacated the locker room with my Seals' duffel bag dragging between my legs.

By sheer coincidence the Berkeley High Yellow Jackets got hot when I left the ballclub; they went on to win their next three games. I ran in to a few of the players during P.E. and we talked about everything that had happened. I was happy for them; they worked hard for coach Wilson and it was paying off. Paul "Squeaky" Daniels took over shortstop from me and did a good job.

The last months of twelve years of public school education were finally upon us; around the time the Oaks would arrive at Seals Stadium—the second week in June—my final grades were going to be due. I had my work cut out if I wanted to end the year with acceptable grades.

These final days were a frenzy of activities. Lettering in baseball for two years, I made certain to get to the Block B Dance, Ditch Day at Searsville Lake, the Senior Ball, and of course graduation. Everything seemed to be happening so fast that it felt like something could easily fall through the cracks. To relieve my mental anguish, I put on music. The soundtrack from "The Great Caruso" is loaded with gut-wrenching arias while Jackie Gleason's romantic ballads helped ease me into a euphoric state of mind. In the solitude of my bedroom I was able to sink into peaceful sleep and dream of what might be.

Back at the ballpark, the Oaks and Seals battled it out to better than average-size crowds. Some older players reminded me to be on my best behavior at this important event while the younger guys gave more encouragement. Red advised me to "Forget the clubhouse and the ball game and concentrate on having a good time while being a gentleman."

My Berkeley High Senior Prom

The creative genius of the Senior Decorations Committee had transformed that tired old gymnasium with flowers. The theme was "Sayonara"—One Last Look. If you were in love or thought you were in love, this scenic splendor magnified all emotion. There must have been close to 300 seniors enjoying Ray Hackett's orchestra as they played the popular love standards of the forties and fifties. Slow dancing invigorated us while we thought about the fact we were going through the final days of this time of our lives.

My last week in Berkeley High was anything but dull. I made it a point to say goodbye to everyone of my teachers, especially giving thanks to Walter Miller and Ray Hernandez for having helped place me in some rather nifty jobs. We marched into our seats in the school auditorium to the surprising music of the "Grand March"

from "Celeste Aida," one of my favorites from the Guisseppi Verdi operas. My
parents rewarded me with a new watch.

The day after graduation, Rocci Giordono and I drove up to Eureka for a doubelheader against the Humboldt Crabs. Our semi-pro team was clobbered in both games and my performance was pathetic. I made a couple of errors and struck out at least three times.

My final report cards arrived on Monday, June 21: 3 A's and 2 C's. I earned C's in Vocational Print and Algebra I, the A's in Driver Education, Physical Education and Work Experience. I started to pull together my transcripts for the Admissions Office at Cal Poly in San Luis Obispo. Bob Roth and I worked out the details to visit the campus in July. No rest for the wicked as I prepared myself for my first day in the Oakland clubhouse, having taken on a second job in professional baseball with Red Adams' Oaks.

10

Off the Field and into the Clubhouse

After the 1953 season, Bob Stevens of the *San Francisco Chronicle* reported on the efforts to keep the Seals franchise in San Francisco. I followed his and other news stories about the sale of the Seals with great interest. Reading Damon Miller's name in the papers, I reflected on our exchange of letters in 1950. The man who made my dreams come true was on the hot seat to come up with the money to run the ballclub and lease Seals Stadium from Paul Fagan. My continued employment and those of my fellow workers was in jeopardy. As September flowed into October, I had to juggle a number of issues that would affect my life, not least of which was whether the Seals would be around in the fall or not. Before granting the franchise, the directors of the PCL needed to review Miller's financial status. The matter would finally be decided at their December meeting.

By early December, Damon Miller had mobilized the greatest effort ever made to keep baseball in San Francisco and had offered the ballclub stock to the public at $10 a share. He was hoping for a positive response. The issue of the stadium lease remained the final sticking point for the league's directors. On December 11, assured of financial solvency, they granted their final approval. Damon Miller became my hero a second time!

On a Friday night in mid-March, the Seals opened the 1954 season once again with a two-week series of major league exhibition games—beginning with the Pittsburgh Pirates. It was my first day back at Seals Stadium, and with the resolution of what would happen to the team finally resolved, I was especially happy to be back. After several years of working at 16th & Bryant, it was a comfort to return each new season, so much so that my school work suffered some. My attitude was that I already had enough credits to graduate and going after ground balls during infield practice sure beat hitting the books.

My assignment for the 1954 season was the same as in the previous year and, once again, I would work with Leo Hughes and Don Rode. Bob Ferguson and Johnny McCormack also returned as batboys; the three of us picked up right where we had left off. We helped Don get his work done for the Seals' first game. There were several returning players and a number of new faces who raised manager Tommy Heath's expectations about the club. Everybody wanted to succeed for Damon Miller and the Little Corporation.

Coming out of spring training, the Seals' infield looked the same as in 1953. George Vico was at first base, Jim Moran at second, Leo Righetti at shortstop and Reno Cheso back at third base: the infield seemed ready. Nini Tornay and Will Tiesiera returned to anchor behind-the-plate-duties. Harlan Clift began his second year assisting Tommy Heath with coaching the hitters, while Myron McCormick was added to coach the outfielders. Bill McCawley, Sal Taormina, Frankie Kalin, Jerry Zuvela, and Al Lyons resumed coverage of the outfield. Some pitchers also returned, including Bill Bradford, Elmer Singleton, Al Lien, Tony Ponce, Bob Muncrief, and Ted Shandor.

Among the new players was one of the funniest guys I ever met: Bobby DiPietro was a natural comedian with an unlimited array of stories. He was also an outstanding ballplayer. Age twenty-six, the right-handed hitter and outfielder was from Louisville

Jim Moran, second baseman and Bob DiPietro, outfielder

85

of the American Association. We also picked up left-handed hitting outfielder Elias Osorio, who at twenty-four had been accomplishing a massive batting average at Carlsbad of the Longhorn League. Among the several new pitchers was right-hander Frank Hiller, a thirty-four year old vet from the New York Giants, and southpaw Adrian Zabala, another Giants vet who was thirty-six.

A number of younger players joined us after spring training. They gave Tommy an opportunity to select from the most promising among them for a shot with the parent club. Among those considered the best were infielders Mike Baxes and Jimmy Westlake; pitchers Jimmy Collins and Audie Malone; and Jose Perez and Tommy Perez (no relation to each other). I was fascinated watching these players compete for the starting lineup and observing how Tommy shuffled them in the roster. During the two weeks of exhibition games, Tommy was able to determine which players would make the team before the season opener set for Tuesday, April 6.

The Seals hosted the Seattle Rainiers who had Artie Wilson and Jackie Tobin returning for another season with a new manager, ex-major leaguer Jerry Priddy. Priddy had a lot of ability and contributed as an infielder as well; he could play every position and pitch. Ray Orteig returned to anchor the catching assignment. Pitchers Al Widmar, Vern Kindsfather, and Steve Nagy returned with several newcomers, including ex-major leaguers Tommy Byrne (from the Yankees), and Gene Bearden (from the Chicago White Sox). Seattle had enough new faces to make it seem like a different ballclub.

I was working with the umpires regularly, including Gil Stratton, a movie actor who played "Cookie" in *Stalag 17*. Occasionally I asked Gil about the movie business; he revealed just enough detail about Hollywood and the actresses he knew to make us feel good and didn't spend too much time on the details—leaving a lot of it to my imagination.

The Seals who came together for the 1954 season were different and perhaps a bit better than previous teams I had known. During the first week of the season, I noticed some obvious improvements. Tommy had them believing in themselves and that was coming across. Only time would tell if we would have a winning team once again. The opening night crowds were larger than usual which promised good things for the Little Corporation. Since money was tight, all of us did everything we could to make it all work. This wasn't an era when we chased down and retrieved foul balls just to toss them into the stands. That time would arrive four decades away when the whole economics of the game would dramatically change.

After the Sunday doubleheader with Seattle, the Seals left town for two weeks: first, they headed to Wrigley Field to play against the Los Angeles Angels, and then back to my side of the Bay, to Oaks Park and Charlie Dressen's ballclub.

On Tuesday, April 27, Bobby Bragan brought his Hollywood Stars to San Francisco. Coming out of the dugout and heading in my direction, was that crazy Carlos Bernier. I still had the glove on my hand from infield practice; I tried to walk away as if I hadn't seen him but it was too late. He grabbed me from behind and asked: "Where are you going?!" Words failed to leave my mouth so we simply shook hands. Then, I noticed someone familiar near the Hollywood dugout; it was another well-known actor, Forrest Tucker, who had accompanied the team to San Francisco. Fans had gathered around him to get his autograph. Although Tucker was someone I had enjoyed watching in several westerns, I would have preferred to have seen Betty Grable or Marilyn Monroe sitting behind—or preferably in front of—the dugout. Things like that were mattering more and more.

Hollywood had one dangerous ballclub and the fans were out to see the Seals do battle with Bragan's boys. Big Jack Phillips, Tommy Saffell, and Dale Long returned with expectations of winning another pennant. The Pirates had sent down southpaws Roger Bowman along with another hot prospect from their farm system, Lino Dinoso. Bragan had created depth in his pitching staff, and had speed on the bases, as well as many guys who could hit the long ball. Doubling as catcher, Bragan alternated with Eddie Malone and Jim Mangan. After the Sunday doubleheader, it was a good thing to see Hollywood leave town. But, the season was still young and a lot could happen when the two teams locked horns again.

I had only a month or so before my graduation when I assumed my position with the Seals would be over; after all, I had watched Buzzy and Bob being let go at the end of their high school years. I wasn't expecting it when Don Rode came to see me down near the dugout prior to the doubleheader. He said he had been thinking that I would make more money working the Visitors Clubhouse and wanted to know if I was interested. "Hell yes," I told him. Then, he said we should get together when the Seals took off for a week.

That was when he could tell me everything that was involved with the new position.

When the Seals left town again, I hopped the Key System bus and the F train to the city of my birth and arrived at the Bay Terminal on my way to 16th & Bryant. I arrived at the Seals Clubhouse where Don Rode was working. He smiled and announced, "Let's get started." He explained the duties and responsibilities of the clubhouse man and assured me that I would enjoy the experience. Chico Norton, head custodian and groundskeeper, joined us and we headed over to the Visitors Clubhouse. It looked like the mirror-image of the Seals Clubhouse with a few notable exceptions. The locker room cubicles were a darker green and there was no carpet on the floor in front of the lockers; the place seemed rather barren. Chico explained the cleaning procedures and Don explained the laundry room. In addition to having responsibility for

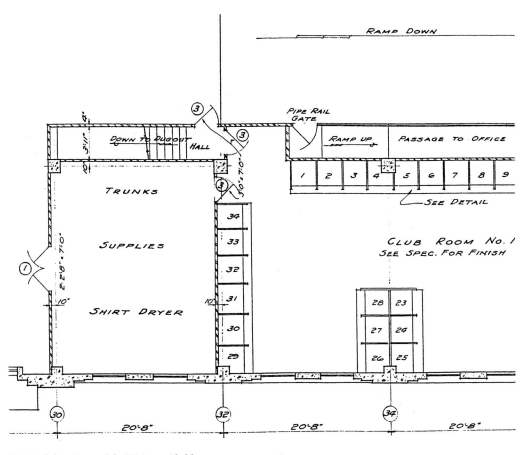

Original drawings of the Visitors Clubhouse, my new assignment

cleaning, washing, and taking care of the toilets and urinals, my job would include buying the goodies for the players to munch and sip on. Also, I would have to make sandwiches on the Sunday doubleheaders to feed the team between the two games.

After my initiation, Don took me to the Hirsch Concession department to reintroduce me to Bill and Jack Cassidy. There, I would need to buy soft drinks, beer, and ice. As I looked into their eyes, I could see dollar signs. I realized the enormous potential to earn far more than my previous three bucks a game. In my new role, I would be off the Seals' payroll and on my own; my ability to earn would have everything to do with how hard I worked and how creative I could be. As I headed back to the Visitors Clubhouse and sat in the quiet empty locker room, I daydreamed a little. On the one hand, I would be giving up putting on a baseball uniform; I would miss being on the field with

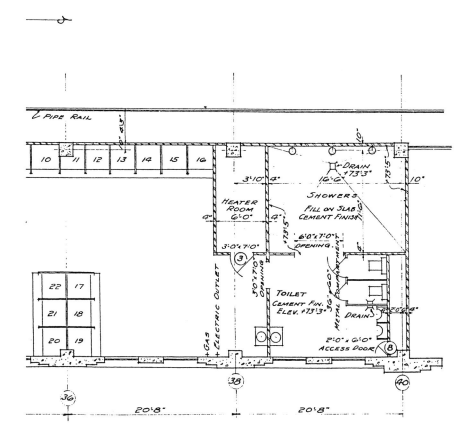

the players and the umpires. On the other, I would make far more money and have the chance to form more direct relationships with everyone who came through those two green doors. I snapped to and started cleaning up the place, following the procedures I had been shown. When I was finished and thoroughly satisfied that the place looked presentable, I start planning for my first visiting team, the Los Angeles Angels. I had just a few days to purchase the goodies before the team arrived.

One afternoon after school, I headed into Oakland to purchase candy, gum, cigarettes, and chewing tobacco at M & M Wholesale Distributors off San Pablo Avenue. On the train ride to San Francisco, I continued my plans. I double-checked the clubhouse, set up my supplies in the room next door, and worked out my behind-the-scenes operation. At Berkeley High, I had used the print shop facilities to create a pad on standard-size paper complete with space for each player's name and any items he might purchase. With my preparations completed, I was ready for the Angels to come to town on May 11.

On Monday, May 10, I rushed into Seals Stadium, empty except for the more than thirty duffel bags the Angels' bus had dropped off on its way to the Alexander Hamilton Hotel. As if I knew what I was doing, I loaded the bags onto the battery-driven cargo carrier that was most often used for the seat cushions; then, I drove up the ramp. The doors to the empty clubhouse were open and I tossed each bag in front of a locker. The players' bags were randomly distributed in front of the lockers, except for the bag of the new trainer, Joe Liscio; this went in his work area. The bags of manager Bill Sweeney and coach Jackie Warner were placed next to each other, in front of and next to the manager's area.

The fun really began as I unloaded the contents of each bag, hanging up the sweatshirts and underwear and placing a pair of shoes on the accompanying bench for polishing. Any item of clothing in need of being laundered got tossed into a pile for the washing machine. I copied Don Rode's method of hanging up the uniforms and baseball caps for ready identification. To put me in a mellow mood, I placed a couple of twelve-inch record albums into the portable player and listened to Lanza's album "The Great Caruso" and the soundtrack of "The Student Prince." (Not too loud since sound carried all too well in the uninhabited locker room.) After shining over thirty pairs of base-ball shoes, I took my break, walking out to the top row of box seats and relaxing in the nearly empty stadium. Harvey and Shorty were going about their chores preparing the field.

After loading up the beverage ice-box with soft drinks and beer, I called it a day and headed back to Berkeley and my parent's home. The ride on the bottom deck of the Bay Bridge allowed me to ponder meeting the Angels' new trainer and many of the players I had known since 1951. Mama's Mexican home cooking satisfied me enough while I told my parents about my day. They were encouraging and pleased that I was doing something I thoroughly enjoyed. I used the remaining time to finish my project for Miss Ernestine Page's Driver Education class: a plan for an overhead rail system that could alleviate congested traffic in the Bay Area. Tomorrow would be a big day, though, so I finally (and peacefully) slipped away into dreamland.

Enthusiastically, I made my way to the Visitors Clubhouse, unlocked the doors, and gave the floor a fresh mopping. When it was dry, the Pine Sol gave off a pleasantly clean aroma, soon to be overlaid with the scent of the fresh Milo coffee I planned to prepare. I transferred each player's name from the official scorebook to my special form and added trainer Joe Liscio, and then I taped the list on the wall next to the beverage container. My supplies—ready to sell to the visiting players—included one carton each of Chesterfield and Lucky Strike cigarettes, Beech Nut chewing tobacco, Wrigley's chewing gum, and "male" and "female" Hershey bars (those with nuts and those without). I picked up two bags of crushed ice from the concession department, dumped them over the soft drinks, and quenched my thirst with a Mission Orange soft drink. Dinner would be a couple of hot dogs and another soda. With my nineteenth birthday just six months away, I avoided the beer, nor did I even have a hankering for it even though I would be sure to buy a case if the Angels won. For now, it was just my orange drink and me.

Three hours before the game and I was done with my work, ready for a nap. Mario Lanza's "Love Songs" and "A Neapolitan Serenade" assisted my entrance into slumber land.

Around 5:30, the door opened. I heard footsteps so I jumped off the trainers' table and prepared to greet Joe Liscio. The new trainer was dressed in a sport coat, slacks, and knit shirt. He shook my hand and with a broad smile, he told me, "You've got quite a place here." With Joe was coach Jackie

Warner, followed by manager Bill Sweeney. It felt like old-home week. Then, somebody yelled, "Where's the coffee?" I told them that I would get right to it and high-tailed it to the coffee maker. As I came back into the room, somebody joked: "Who'd you pay off to get this job?" I stood there laughing with them. Liscio turned to the manager and coach and said, "This is like being in the major leagues." Joe came to Los Angeles from the Philadelphia Phillies. I was astounded and pleased simultaneously. Joe took me aside and told me to make myself scarce when the manager called for a meeting in about an hour. After making the coffee and marking 10 cents after each name of the person who took some, I watched as the door opened again and several players walked in.

Outfielder Bob Usher and infielder Bud Hardin said they were happy to see me, but I didn't recognize half-a-dozen new players including second baseman Gene Mauch and outfielder-infielder Tommy Brown. Brown stood out because of his exceptional good looks. Three pitchers were familiar: Calvin McLish, Bob Spicer, and big John Pyecha. Each one found his way to one of the lockers. I had one week to learn something about each player because in addition to whatever they purchased from me, I would be charging them clubhouse dues of $1.25 each. The process of getting to know them had just begun.

I learned a lot from listening and moving about the clubhouse during the season. I heard what the men of that generation liked and disliked. Right away outfielder Max West told the younger players to dress warmly as temperatures would drop before the game ended. He also told them that unlike Wrigley Field, at Seals Stadium they would have to hit the ball with greater authority. Classic clubhouse chatter included exchanges about San Francisco's hot spots like the International Settlement, downtown jazz joints, and the movie houses on Market Street. They also talked about the celebrities, such as umpire Gil Stratten who played in *Stalag 17*, Marlon Brando who was starring in *Viva Zapata* or actors in the MGM musicals showing at the Lowes-Warfield. One of the players described the attractive usherettes and that kicked off comments about the beautiful cosmopolitan women of San Francisco. Liscio broke their concentration by mentioning the best places to eat in town: Original Joe's, Bernstein's Fish Grotto, and Tommy's Joint. Before long, I had to make my exit which gave Sweeney a chance to go over the game and their opponents—the Seals hitters and pitchers.

I used this time to go down to the dugout and yell something encouraging to batboy Johnny McCormack and some of the Seals. I was quickly adjusting to my new assignment. After nine innings the Angels came back to the clubhouse to reflect on their loss; Sweeney quickly changed his clothes and headed back to the hotel. After Liscio finished working on the arms of one of the pitchers, he too showered, changed, and then departed with Jackie Warner, while I stayed behind to clean the mud from everyone's spikes, gather the towels in a big bundle for the linen company, and tidy up. Tired as hell, I still made certain to shower, lock up, and hope that one of the East Bay guys would be around to give me a ride home. On this particular night, I was lucky: Bill Bradford had stuck around to get a rub down from Leo Hughes. As we drove back across the Bay Bridge, we talked about the Seals' victory and my new job.

The Seals were having their way with the Angels—a new experience for me. Through my first three seasons with the club, they had certainly not been beating down the doors of the first division. The visiting Angels—who weren't drinking much celebratory beer—were open and honest talking about the home team's relatively new success. We all noticed how many fans were turning out, too. Max West had credited Tommy Heath for turning the ballclub around.

In the middle of Friday night's game, I chased down Don Rode to ask if I could stay overnight in the stadium rather than make the trip back to Berkeley just to return early on Saturday. He said he would talk with Leo and a little later he came to give me the good news. He cautioned me to keep the door locked from the inside of the First-Aid Station as the "ghost of Seals' past" was known to roam the inside concourse. I assured him that I would keep the lights on.

I don't remember if the Angels won that night but there were guys nursing their bottles of beer before they went over to old man Stanfel's Double Play, the bar across the street. I was working like hell to get the place in shape, eavesdropping as Joe Liscio talked with pitcher Bob Spicer who was on the rubbing table. By and by the place emptied out; I showered and made it over to the Seals Clubhouse. Don was drinking a beer and offered me one, which I declined, opting instead for a Coke. He's got a mischievous look on his face and I began to wonder what kind of outrage he was planning. Before long we left the clubhouse and he dropped me off at the First-Aid Station with a wink in his eye.

At half-past midnight, Chico Norton stopped by to tell me that the janitors had finished their rounds. He echoed Don Rode when he reminded me to keep the door locked. After everyone was gone, I went to survey the concourse from the third-base and first-base corners of the stadium. There were a couple of lights on overhead, just enough to prevent total darkness. I wasn't in a hurry to go to bed, but finally I returned to the First-Aid Station and closed and locked the door behind me. As I slipped into the tidy little bed, I could hear traffic coming down Bryant Street. Then, something happened: I was out like a light into the deepest of sleeps.

I didn't wake up until seven or eight o'clock the next morning when I heard voices and footsteps and could see a thin sliver of daylight slip under the door. I opened it in time to see several of the janitors getting ready for the day . . . my clue to do likewise. I rushed over to the Visitors Clubhouse, showered and shaved and walked around the corner to Potrero Avenue where there was a coffee shop owned by a Greek gentleman. After a hearty breakfast with good strong coffee, I could carry on a short conversation with the owner. He remembered me coming in for a hot sandwich and told me that the Seals looked better this year.

Back at the clubhouse, I launched into the ritual of preparations for that day's game which included making the arrangements for sandwiches for Sunday's doubleheader. I called my mother to let her know that everything was okay and told her that I would be home that night. Next, I called Serge Ottino of Ottino's Delicatessen in West Berkeley to order the ingredients for approximately thirty-five sandwiches. He tells me to stop by after the game and pick out what I want and he'll put everything together.

After the game, Serge and I go over the menu and the supplies I would need for twenty sandwiches of baked Virginia ham, some with Monterey jack cheese, and fifteen Molinari salami and cheese sandwiches on sour dough rolls. He carefully wrapped up the ingredients and told me how to make the sandwiches: Don't overdo the mayonnaise and be careful with French's Mustard. Everything was in a big shopping bag and there were a few items I would need to refrigerate. That night, I took in a movie to see Elizabeth Taylor and Vittorio Gassman in *Rhapsody* at the United Artists theatre.

Although Saturday's crowd at Seals Stadium was larger than usual—an obvious sign of the Seals' latest string of victories—Sunday brought out the biggest crowd of the week who had come to cheer the Seals on. I was enjoying every bit of the struggle between the Angels and us. Then it dawned on me to question just who I was rooting for? If the Angels won, they might be in a good mood and remember me as they paid their bills. During the break between the two games, the sandwiches were clearly a big hit in the Visitors Clubhouse. As it turned out, the Seals took both games. The Angels returned to the clubhouse, showered, and changed clothes.

As they prepared to leave the clubhouse and head for the bus parked in front of the lobby, each player approached me in front of the General Store, and asked how much they owed me? I broke it gently as some leaned over to hear what the player in front was being charged. The process was simple: I reviewed the tally sheet where each had marked down his purchases, then tallied it in my head and added $1.25 for clubhouse dues. They accepted my total and added a tip, whatever they felt was appropriate. Then, I thanked them and we talked about their next trip to San Francisco. After the last player left the clubhouse, I closed the door and parked myself at the manager's desk. I took the sheet with their entries and tallied up my earnings: over $150, most or all of it in paper money. My wallet swelled to its full capacity. When I subtracted what I spent for the sandwiches, beer and soft drinks, and the supplies for the General Store, I had cleared over $100. Happy days are here again!

I spent most of my earnings but set aside enough to cover my supplies for the next Seals' homestand. My wardrobe needed updating, shoes and items for graduation which would be coming up. I made my first attempt at creating a budget which seemed like an exercise in futility although I gave it my best shot as I recalled Doc Hughes' sign near the rubbing table: "You're through . . . ."

The next Seals road trip was to Portland and further north to Seattle. They won four straight in Oregon as a result of Tommy changing the lineup to include several of the younger players. Before the week was over, the Seals were beginning to see daylight for the first time as they rose out of the cellar.

For Memorial Day, the Portland Beavers came to San Francisco to play a holiday doubleheader. I had to pay a quick visit to Ottino's Delicatessen. By this time, the Seals were in second place and I could see droves of fans arriving early. I wondered what all the fuss was about. Tommy had replaced George Vico at first base with Jimmy Westlake, kept Jim Moran at second base, had Mike Baxes spell Leo Righetti at shortstop, and alternated Reno Cheso with Baxes and Righetti at the hot corner. Merv Donahue joined Nini Tornay and Will Tiesiera behind the plate and the twenty year old kids didn't stop there. Dave Melton joined Jerry Zuvela in the outfield while Audie Malone and Marshall Epperson augmented the pitching staff. This new youthful exuberance caused Bob Stevens of the *San Francisco Chronicle* to dub the new Seals as The Kiddie Kar Express!

Clay Hopper also had made some changes although there were a number of last year's regulars who had come back for another season. Former Seals' pitchers Bill Boemler and John "Butch" Tierney had joined big Bob Alexander, Glenn Elliott, and Red Adams. Alexander, in addition to being a strong right-handed pitcher was quite a card. His teammates urged me to ask for a demonstration of a trick he did with all 52 cards in a deck. That was old as dirt if that's the trick they were talking about. By the end of the week, I caught him at the tail-end of something pretty interesting. I pressed him on this so-called trick the next time they come to town.

Frankie Austin and Eddie Basinski continued to work well together, executing double plays when the opportunity presented itself. Dino Restelli put in another season for the Beavers playing the outfield and hitting the long ball. Jim Gladd and Berkeley High sensation of the early forties Joe Rossi held down the catching assignments. I wasted no time telling Rossi that working the clubhouse cost me the varsity shortstop position at BHS. He looked me square in the eyes and said, "You're kidding?" We got along just fine although he regularly made fun of my nose, asking me that tired line, "Are you sucking on a banana?" Even though Joe had a horn that rivaled Billy Martin, I held my tongue. Although Portland had many interesting ballplayers, most were having

Right-handed pitcher Bob Alexander

a very difficult year. That might have been part of why I liked them so much. That and their good story-telling trainer, Tip Berg.

During this week-long series, I made a catastrophic blunder, one that damn near ruined the clubhouse and cost me my job. It was an afternoon of the Thursday night game and I had left the coffee pot on while I went across the street for a sandwich with Chico Norton. When I came back, I smelled smoke while walking up the ramp toward the clubhouse. Smoke and flames greeted us when we opened the doors. There was a fire burning with great intensity. Although it was confined to the storage room it was not far from the chemical compounds used by the janitors. Chico and I tried to douse it with ice water from the soft drink machine which had little effect. I ran into the manager's locker and called the fire department. Within five minutes, a huge red fire truck pulled into the stadium's lobby. Several firemen jumped down to investigate. I met them halfway down the ramp as they were hauling out their water hoses. I showed them the way to the clubhouse. Within minutes, the fire was out. The fire chief took me to the side and told me to be more careful. Then, he and his crew left.

Not long afterwards, Ruth Merrill of the front office called the clubhouse to ascertain the damage. I told her it was minimal and described what had happened. She told me that she would be sending Shorty, the groundskeeper, over to see me. I didn't know what to think.

I had foolishly placed a two-burner electrical unit on top of a large box of paper cups. One of the coils ignited. Shorty walked into the now cleared-out clubhouse and asked what had happened, then he instructed me to follow him. I didn't know what to expect as we entered a nearby storage area where we picked up a glass storage case where I could showcase the goodies I had bought. It also provided a place to set down the portable hot plate for making coffee, leaving enough room for sugar, cream, cups and plastic spoons. It gave the little room the appearance of a small general store. I turned on my creative juices and painted a 15 X 18 inch sign, "Ye old General Store," listing the items sold and their prices. After taping it above, I was once again ready for business.

An hour later trainer Tip Berg arrived, asking "What's cooking?" After I told him what had happened, he laughed maniacally. When pay day came after the Sunday doubleheader, I was rewarded with compliments as the players paid up and included generous tips. What a week! Next, the Oaks would be coming to Seals Stadium and there would be a Senior Ball at Berkeley High. It would cause me to miss the Friday night game but I didn't think the players would mind too much.

The Little General, Charlie Dressen, brought our rivals into San Francisco for a seven-game series. Jesse "Red" Adams was surprised to see what I had done to the Visitors Clubhouse. The melodic tunes of Jackie Gleason with Bobby Hackett's trumpet were playing softly in the corner, giving off a subtle but serene effect. The clubhouse had been scrubbed to an antiseptic cleanliness, the heater was on, and the General Store was all set up with the smell of fresh coffee filling the air. The smile on his face said it all. He told me that he had been clubhouse man for the Mission Reds in the next door clubhouse a long time ago and that I had done wonders to the place.

Many familiar faces were now arriving. I had worked for some of them when I had been their batboy; they were startled and surprisingly happy to see me. Broad smiles and strong handshakes. Johnny Jorgensen asked who I had to pay off in order to get this job. Pitchers George Bamberger and Chris Van Cuyk wanted a cup of coffee and acted like they hadn't seen the sign-in sheet, so I reminded them. Neither Charlie Beamon nor Ernie Broglio recognized me from high school baseball which made it easier to maintain the respect and consideration I showed to everyone. It was great to renew my old acquaintances with Red and the players, and although it was noisy as hell in the clubhouse with plenty of excitement in the air, it was comfortable too. Both Bay Area teams appeared evenly matched finally.

Before Charlie Dressen gathered the players for their pre-game meeting, I discretely left to have dinner: a tubular steak and soft drink from the closest restaurant in town, the concession across the hall. The fans were pouring in early to get a good seat; I found an empty corner in the box seats close to the dugout. Joan Stack, the usherette for this area, told me to vacate the area when the fans came in to find their seats. I managed to dine comfortably while watching the young Seals take their infield practice followed by the batboys. My mind wandered to an earlier time when coach Joe Sprinz ran Buzzy Casazza, Bobby Rodriguez, and me through this pre-game ritual. Then, I heard several members of the Oaks coming down to the dugout to get their first peak at the Seals—my signal to get back to the clubhouse and help out Red.

I took advantage of an almost empty clubhouse while Red worked on one of the pitchers to let him know that I would not be working on Friday night because of the Senior Prom. I assured him that I could get most of the work done the night before and come in earlier on Friday if he thought it was necessary. Red doesn't push the issue; he tells me that he will take care of it and not to worry. Later Don Rode lets me know that he can get one of the batboys to give me a hand. With a grin on his face, he tells me that "any one of them would only be too happy to manage your General Store." Oh well, that's show business.

A few days later, trainer Red Adams told me that I was doing a good job. Their home clubhouse man had a career change, so Red asked me if I would like the job. I told him I would. He said I could start anytime in the next two weeks as the Seals would be on the road. I had a couple of prior arrangements, next Friday night's graduation, and next Saturday's semi-pro game in Eureka. Red said the following week would be okay when the Portland Beavers come to Oakland. How about that? Without trying I got another job. Doing precisely what I like and closer to home. The extra money would be useful for college.

"Luck is the residue of design." With Branch Rickey's words in my mind I took the Number 72 Key System bus to Park Street and San Pablo Avenue in Emeryville, the home of the Oakland Oaks. Wednesday, June 22 would be the start of a short and memorable adventure, as I went to work for Red Adams and the Oakland baseball club. They were about to host Clay Hopper's Portland Beavers for a weeklong series. The clubhouse was smaller and easier to keep clean but more importantly I was now in the historic domain of Billy Martin and Casey Stengel's Nine Old Men. Working with Red would be a pleasurable experience.

Meanwhile, during the following week, the Seals entertained the Sacramento Solons. Now managed by Gene Desaultes who was later replaced by pitcher Tony Freitas, Sacramento had jumped off to a good start and was battling Hollywood for first place by the first month of the season. When they arrived at Seals Stadium on June 29, we were both fighting for second and third place in the standings. It looked like the year we might both come out winners; we might even escape out of second division. By the time July rolled around, things would really be heating up on the field.

Sacramento was an improved ballclub. They had four players who could hit with consistency: Nippy Jones, Bob Dillinger, Joe Brovia, and Hank Schenz. Chick Pieretti continued to pace the pitchers, along with a wickedly fast flame-thrower, the right-hander Al Cicotte. Oh my, he could throw that baseball; when he was *on* he was truly dangerous. For Sacramento's first trip of the season, the team seemed to have a lot of fun jumping up and down in the first division. Trainer Mike Chambers was good to work with; he placed few demands on me except to make some recommendations about my choice of records. He liked nice and easy. I had a good week with them. For the first time, they came in flying high and in a relaxed state of mind and it seemed they knew what they had to do to stay in the running. The Seals posed a problem. Come Sunday afternoon they were all quite generous when paying their bills. Except Chet Johnson: he paid his bill but jumped all over me in a fun-loving way as if he was testing my ability to laugh at myself. After Carlos Bernier, this was nothing.

Lefty O'Doul brought his high-flying San Diego Padres into town next, the last of the seven visiting club's first trips to San Francisco. The Padres were knocking everybody down. They had four guys who were ripping the cover off of the ball: Earl Rapp, Dick Sisler, Milt Smith, and Harry Elliott. Ex-Seal southpaw Lloyd Dickey was having one of his best years, as was Bob Kerrigan and Eddie Erautt. Trainer Les Cook kept everybody in sound condition and razzed me with his colorful stories. Like the one about the fellow who gave his young wife an elephant egg for a wedding present then mentioned that she should spend some time sitting on it to warm it so it could hatch. Three days pass and she screams at her husband when they're both in bed: "I think it's hatched because I can feel the trunk!" Whenever there was a dull moment in the clubhouse or dugout, Les was there to liven things up.

It may have been on this trip that Lefty brought his young son into the clubhouse. My profits started to dwindle watching the kid go after the candy bars and soft drinks, but then I remembered what Lefty had done for me and the Seals franchise. It was worth a fractional loss.

I can't tell you who the big tippers were but a winning ballclub, when everyone was in good spirits, always worked to my benefit. Lloyd Dickey congratulated my job in the clubhouse; when Earl Rapp and Milt Smith jumped in to say something similar, I felt like I had really accomplished something. My sandwiches and music were a hit with the players and with Lefty too. "Kid, you've come a long way. Stay with it and don't let anybody stiff 'ya: If they do, you tell me."

Throughout the rest of the season, I traveled back and forth between Seals Stadium and Oaks Park. I thought about buying an old jalopy to help my commute but I was trying to save something for college. After the last San Francisco game, I rode home with Jim Moran. Tommy had taken the Kiddie Kar Express into the first division by season's end. Leo Hughes and Don Rode finally had the best reason to celebrate.

11

Red Adams, the Oaks, and Me

At about age ten, after the end of the Big War in 1945, I attended my very first professional ball game: it was at Oaks Park. Located in Emeryville, California—a small urban municipality between southwest Berkeley and west Oakland—the Oakland Oaks and I were practically neighbors. By the time, I entered adolescence, I had to choose the team I would root for. Remembering that I was, after all, a native San Franciscan, I tipped my cap to the Seals. Of course, this put me into direct conflict with not just the kids in my school and neighborhood, but all of West Berkeley, or so it seemed. There were many heated exchanges especially during the 1948 pennant race when the classic rivalry reached fever pitch. The Seals and the Oaks were evenly matched that year, fighting for first place up to the very last day of the season. Casey Stengel's Oaks—including his infamously tenacious Nine Old Men and Billy Martin—deservedly won the pennant.

I used to have to argue my way onto the Columbus School playground whenever the neighborhood kids talked about which team was the best: the San Francisco Seals or the Oakland Oaks. From as far back as I could remember, my pals kidded me about rooting for a "pennant winner." I just kept telling them "wait until next year." Unfortunately, that had become my response for several years in a row. And during those years, I had to acknowledge the victorious Oakland Oaks and congratulate my jubilant friends.

By the time Red Adams picked me to come and work for him, I had mostly grown out of my view of the Oaks as "the enemy," though I dared not reveal this to anyone. Instead, something in me wanted to keep the rivalry going. Inwardly, I knew the Oaks had a better team but I had become skillful at avoiding the truth by camouflaging myself in the loyalty I owed to the Seals who, after all, had even given me my first job in baseball.

I didn't have too much difficulty swallowing my pride during the first few seasons I worked for the Seals, but when the opportunity came to earn more money by going "down the street" to the Home of the Oaks in nearby Emeryville, my values were not too difficult to compromise although my inward bias would always be in favor of the Seals. The experience of being the Seals' Visitors' batboy had already primed me to be gracious and show respect to opposing teams and to individual players. This was largely responsible for helping me cope with the neighborhood rivalries that could easily erupt into yelling, leading to pushing and shoving.

The Oaks looked noticeably different from the Seals in their New York Yankees' styled pinstriped uniforms. Instead, the Oaks wore cream-colored uniforms with a distinctive Gothic "O" on their caps during home games. On the left side of their jerseys, the "O" was outlined in red. These players were idolized by most of the teenagers in my neighborhood and throughout the Bay Area. We followed their games described by Bud Foster, first on KLX and then on KROW radio. Most of us collected the baseball cards sponsored by Remar Bread, Smith's Clothiers, Mothers' Cookies, and the Signal Oil Company.

So many Oakland players lived in our communities and were our role models. They encouraged kids to get out and play ball. After World War II, West Berkeley's Augie Galan of the 1933 Seals—a longtime player with the Cincinnati Reds—and several Oaks players, worked out at

Red Adams, Oaks trainer

nearby James Kenney Park. We couldn't get enough baseball, playing variations of the game on the Columbus School playground or at Kenney.

Many of the older boys in the neighborhood were already playing ball at Berkeley High, including Ruben De Alba, Dick Dawson, Emil Fuhrman, Choke Mejia, Howard Noble, Eddie Leneve, Babe Van Heuit, and, oh yes, Billy Martin. These Kenney Park alumni eventually all signed professional baseball contracts. The game was so popular after the war that nearly every community had at least one semi-pro team. Every city bordering Oakland had teams that played each other on Saturdays and Sundays in all the neighborhood ballparks; they always attracted sizable crowds. The same thing happened across the Bay.

When the Oaks were home, pre-teenagers Rocci Giordano, Don Capellino, Mario Fraire, and I regularly made the three-mile trip to Oaks Park on Saturdays. We rode either the Number 72 Key System bus or took our bicycles to San Pablo Avenue and Park Street, then walked or rode one more block west to Watts Street behind the Oaks' right field bleachers. There were no ticket booths in right field (well, not exactly). Around nine or ten o'clock in the morning, we hoisted ourselves up into a hole about twenty-five inches around and crawled into an almost empty ballpark. The Emeryville Police probably looked the other way rather than snatch us up and haul us back through the locked gate. Once, after sneaking into the park, I saw Howard Storm, one of the West Berkeley kids who was working as the Oaks' batboy. He looked at us and with utter disbelief shook his head. His look meant approval to us. Then, we hauled our sneaky selves down to the first-base side before the usherettes arrived . . . all the way down to the Oaks' dugout. One of the players, either Brooks Holder or Ray Hamrick, would stop to greet us and sign his autograph. Each of us had brought along a sandwich in a brown bag and a jar of iceless Kool-Aid because we rarely had money for a soda. Instead we nursed our homemade sugary drinks and yelled off our fool heads. Although we always brought along our baseball gloves to catch fouls, all we usually caught was the warm summer breeze.

Once the game started, we were able to find some area in the stands where the usherettes or the Emeryville Police would not bother us. Capellino's Uncle Felix was a fireman and his presence at the firehouse next door gave us some sense of protection. The coziness of the Oaks' wood stadium encouraged a lot of kids to find ways to sneak in.

Oaks Park was a compact ballpark constructed in 1913; after four decades it underwent necessary improvements. When he surmised that there would be a surge of fans after the war, owner Brick Laws upgraded the stadium in hopes of cashing in on the national post-war economic boom and baseball's renewed popularity. Oaks Park got a fresh coat of green paint inside and out while the seating areas were highlighted in red or red-orange. The light poles in the third and first-base stands were moved back to make room for additional seating. The left and right-field fences—including the back fence of the right-field bleachers—were painted with colorful advertisements placed by local merchants and hotels. The clubhouses were moved from center field and placed under the stands near home plate to give the hitters an uncluttered green background behind the pitchers.

Like Paul Fagan, Brick Laws also hired attractive young women to serve as ushers, taking over the jobs once held by scruffy older men who had done the work since the turn of the century. Most of us saw this innovation as a great improvement.

The neighborhoods around Oaks Park were mostly residential, with some light and heavy manufacturing factories and warehouses sprinkled here and there. The visiting teams stayed at the California Hotel on San Pablo six or seven blocks south of MacArthur Boulevard in West Oakland. Across the street was the El Rey Theater featuring, I'm told, some of the finest burlesque shows on the West Coast. The poor visiting players were hardly in a fighting mood come game time. (I'm exaggerating a little). After World War II, the visiting teams stayed at the Hotel Leamington in downtown Oakland. Emeryville had an anything-but-dull reputation and a history of serving up food and intoxicating spirits in houses of ill-repute during the good old days, when the nights weren't so bad either.

Because of the ballpark's location in a semi-industrial neighborhood, there were many great and inexpensive food and drink establishments nearby. Two outstanding Italian restaurants, Angelo's and Ravazza's, attracted fans and players alike. The Oaks Corner, located across the street from the ballclub's ticket offices, featured excellent Hofbrau-style food, while Nell's Diner up the block specialized in American country cooking. Much like Stanfel's Double Play across from Seals Stadium, the Oaks Corner featured all kinds of liquid libation and good food. Eighteen going on nineteen-years old,

I had yet to discover the enormous benefits of a fully-supplied, elbow-bending, rip-snorting bar room: a pleasure that was still slightly over the horizon.

The Emeryville Fire Station was located on the same block where the two Italian restaurants did their booming business; it was situated so that the back door had easy access to the grandstand section near the park's home plate, primed to respond to an occasional fire. The Police Station at the corner of Park and Hollis streets supplied a cadre of officers who took their positions in the ballpark's walkways. Few arrests were ever made although there were a number of gamblers gathered in certain areas exchanging mythical fortunes.

To the west, past the Oaks Corner and over the left-field fence, stood the two-story structure of the American Rubber Company. Once in a while a hitter with pretty good power would send one into the windows or maybe on top of the roof for a tape-measured homerun. Del Monte Packing Company had a packing shed about three blocks down Park Street which employed hundreds of men and women as seasonal workers. You could smell the tomatoes over the right-field bleachers during the summer packing season. French's Mustard had a manufacturing plant a couple of blocks away, and, not to be overshadowed by Del Monte, they did their best to fill evenings with distinctive and inviting aromas. Day or night during the canning and bottling season, you could inhale the best of Del Monte and French's products lingering in the air.

North from Oaks Park to the next major intersection on San Pablo Avenue was Stanford Street to the east and Powell Street to the west. On the northwest corner was Strom's Clothing Store, a favorite of the big-and-tall ballplayers. Across the street from Strom's, on the northeast corner, the Golden Gate Theater featured Hollywood's latest. The more popular movie houses were located in downtown Oakland and included the Fox-Oakland, the Paramount, the T&D, and the Roxie. Moving south on the avenue there were a number of fine men's clothing shops polka-dotting the neighborhood, and on the north side of the park you would find South Berkeley Creamery, Emery High School, and the Key System Corporation Yard.

Due to an unusual quirk in the 1954 PCL schedule, my first work day for the Oaks began Wednesday, June 22, when the Portland Beavers came in for a six-game series. It was excitingly different to walk through the unmanned front gate of Oaks Park. First, I reported to Red Adams at the Oaks clubhouse, located beneath the wooden stands behind home plate. I showed up three hours before game time and before the players arrived. Red was the former clubhouse man of the Mission Reds. He told me that I should know what to do and spent several minutes acquainting me with the layout. It was a smaller clubhouse than what I was used to at Seals Stadium; this made it easier to keep clean. . .or so I thought. I began sweeping and antiseptically mopping the cement floor, following the same routine I had developed at the Visitors Clubhouse across the bay. When I was through cleaning, I located the soft drink and beer container and purchased several cases of the more popular sodas (Coca Cola, 7-Up and Hire's Root Beer), as well as beer and crushed ice, from the concession department down the hall.

Manager Charlie Dressen and his 1954 Oakland Oaks

After shining all of the shoes and placing the sanitary socks over them, I anxiously waited for the home team and those young and old familiar faces. Red was busy setting up his work station; it included boxes of eggs that he brought for the players from his neighborhood in Petaluma. He placed the

Official Score Book

Lee Susman

OAKLAND OAKS
1954   PRICE 15 CENTS

fragile merchandise on shelves in a separate room which also served as the office for manager Charlie Dressen—the "Little General" as he was discretely called by some of his players.

Mr. Dressen and I got along well as long as I worked quietly around him. He always seemed to have a lot on his mind just trying to get his players focused and headed for the first division. His reputation as a winning manager preceded his return to Oakland. Dressen served the Oaks previously in 1949 and '50 when the team came in second and first place those years. From 1951 through 1953, he left to manage the Brooklyn Dodgers all the way to their two and almost three pennants. Bobby Thompson of the New York Giants beat him with that "Shot heard 'round the world," cheating him out of the '51 pennant. I knew I was working in the shadow of greatness and for that reason it wasn't too much of a sacrifice to not play my portable phonograph in this clubhouse. Anyway, most of the time the place was crowded. Dressen kept to himself next to the eggs.

The Oaks' coach was Dressen's teammate from the Dodgers, Harry "Cookie" Lavagetto from the Berkeley and Oakland border area. Between the two of them, they knew baseball.

I knew many of the players already, but they seemed surprised to see me in their domain as they walked through the clubhouse door. Surprise turned to teasing—the team's way of initiating me into their club. Most delighted in making me squirm a little. Some complained about having to pay for the items I sold or for the clubhouse dues. When they realized how serious I was about my "business," several of them broke out into maniacal laughter. With four years in the league, I should have developed a thicker skin by that point and gotten used to the ironical and often unexpected verbal punches. After the Sunday doubleheaders, my efforts and the baked Virginia ham sandwiches were paid for with friendly and generous aplomb.

It was difficult to work in the tighter and more cluttered quarters. Apparently the size of the ballpark translates to the success of the club. With the outfield fences within easy reach, everybody had a chance to hit homeruns, with the home town favorites hitting more. The Seals had a bigger home with the outfield fences beyond the reach of many players. A homerun in Seals Stadium was a monumental accomplishment and required a different strategy; hitters

Preceding page: A classic Lee Susman cartoon cover for the Oakland Oaks

there had to rely on driving the ball between the outfielders for extra bases, and good pitching helped.

The ability to keep every player in shape often meant the difference between a winning and losing ballclub. Red worked effectively, mostly on the pitchers, rubbing the aches and pains out of arms, backs, and legs. As he worked, he listened and talked with the athlete on his rubbing table. Red was super interesting; he had a quiet voice, a stern look, a raised eyebrow, and an engaging smile. Everyone seemed to trust him and enjoy his company. And, he didn't have a mean bone in his body. He knew many people in the area of Oaks Park. During Friday night games, Red would send me over to Nell's Country Diner for her tuna sandwiches. Not necessarily my favorite but Nell's were darn near excellent! Their lunch time menu—with its great meat loaf plate with mashed potatoes—was well worth a trip.

As though the clubhouse were not already crowded, Red frequently welcomed people from the community to visit when the players were out on the field. Some high school baseball coaches would come by and bend Red's ears about a hot prospect. Red, in his other role as scout for the ballclub, kept tabs on a number of high school players, following games in Alameda County and in the Oakland Athletic Leagues. He monitored the progress of Billy Martin at both James Kenney Park and in high school. My down-the-street classmate Rocci Giordano had several good seasons pitching for Berkeley High and was invited to workout with the team; later, he met with Brick Laws. Eventually, Rocci signed a contract with the Boston Red Sox. George Powles, the outstanding McClymonds High school baseball coach, came by to see if Charlie Beamon was making the adjustment. Many of George's varsity ballplayers ended up signing professional contracts, including Frank Robinson and Jesse Gonder. Bob Zuk, who managed an Oakland semi-pro team, was another of Red's regular visitors, keeping him informed about an athlete who might make it in professional ball.

Abe Rose, owner of Abe's Sporting Goods near the Leamington Hotel, was another clubhouse chum who came by with his top line of sporting goods, equipment, and uniforms for Red to take a look at. I sat down and listened as they talked about the great looking, high-quality merchandise. Mr. Rose knew precisely what Red would be interested in and always elaborated on how the money would be well-spent. Red would be glued to the discussion while fiddling with his chin as he contemplated his budget restrictions. The Oaks' trainer was the epitome of kindness and consideration, always available to hear somebody's story.

George McDermott, former infielder with the Mission Reds, was another visitor. George grew up in West Berkeley and years later his two sons, Mickey and Frank, worked for Red as batboys. Frank and I played semi-pro ball during the winter with Guy's Drugs.

I made it a point to connect with the Visitors Clubhouse man. I called him Eddie because I thought I heard someone call him that. He never told me his name. Every time I asked, he laughed and asked me to keep guessing. "Eddie" was inconvenienced by a speech impediment and a slight limp, but he was built like a weight-lifter. When I wasn't looking, he would sneak up on me and wrap me in his super muscular arms, then lift me off the floor—laughing the whole time. Aside from avoiding his horrific handshakes, he was fun to work with. When we had the time, we spent a good half hour evaluating the visiting clubs and listing the "good tippers." He was a hard worker with a positive attitude and a keen sense of humor.

The head groundskeeper had a Scandinavian accent and stern demeanor. His sense of order was put to perfect use maintaining the park's playing surfaces. Several locals worked with him part-time to keep the field in tip-top shape. He discouraged the batboys and me from getting on the infield before the Oaks took their batting practice.

The batboys were like Red's step-children and I let them scurry around the clubhouse without getting in their way. I focused on my job and getting to know the players from this new perspective. During the '54 season, several players wore plastic liners in the inside of their caps, should a "wild pitch" get away from some irate pitcher. The first cap I saw that had been doctored like this was Johnny "Spider" Jorgensen's. Shortstop Russ Rose also had one; I asked him about it. He told me that he was such a fearless hitter that he knew several pitchers were out to get him. I took him so seriously that when he saw my concerned expression, he laughed. That's when outfielder and pinch-hitter Bill Howerton told me not to believe anything Russ said. First baseman Jim Marshall—lovingly called the "Wick" by some of his teammates—was another delightful guy. He had fun in the clubhouse: well, they all did until the manager showed up.

From my perspective, the most interesting member on the team was Lorenzo "Piper" Davis. He was one of three Negroes on the team, along with pitcher Charlie Beamon and third baseman Bob Wilson (although when I arrived in July, Charlie and Bob were not on the team). Piper was a veteran of the Negro Leagues and the PCL; at thirty-seven, he was still making his mark as an extraordinarily gifted athlete, accomplished in basketball (with the Harlem Globetrotters) as well as in baseball. He was the first Negro to sign a contract with the Boston Red Sox. He exhibited so much talent that playing just one position wasn't an option. I had the sense that Piper had seen and heard a lot, and held in his emotions. Still, he gave everything he had to make Oakland a winning team, channeling his energies into each game. I still remember the hard slide into Seals' pitcher Bill Boemler one day in July of 1952, and the ensuing fight that helped enflame the forty-year rivalry between the Oaks and Seals.

Oakland Oaks' owner Brick Laws tried an assortment of creative gimmicks to attract fans. He had trickster comedian and ex-ballplayer Jackie Price stage an exhibition of ball-handling maneuvers, including catching balls thrown to him as he hung upside down in the middle of the infield. He would gather three batboys and put three balls in his hand, then toss them at once in three different directions. It excited the crowd when each batboy caught a separate ball. The antics delighted the crowd and players alike.

The Oaks also sponsored "winning-ticket contests" to award a fan with a case of Havoline motor oil or an AM radio. Oakland players hitting a home-run in a certain area in the park also won a prize. Then there was the Cowboy, Allen "Two Gun" Gettel, the right-handed pitcher who rode into the ballpark on a horse, guns "twirling and a-blazing" with noise. Not only was he a colorful figure, but he also had a pretty good year on the mound. The Oaks did whatever it took to bring out the fans and they did it with what turned out to be a first division ballclub.

The Oaks tolerated me working out in the infield before a game—after completing my clubhouse work, that is. I suited up and patrolled the area between third and second base, trying to catch anything hit near me. I did fine until big Chris Van Cuyk, the left-handed pitcher, urged me to move over between first and second base. He said he would hit me some ground balls, calculated to make me a better infielder. He had mastered the art of the fungo bat and hit me ground balls that would take a high short hop in front of me thus challenging my abilities. I think more got through me than I caught, but within time, I got the idea. He was trying to have fun helping me, and it worked.

The relationship between West Berkeley and the Oaks had a lot of history and was mutually beneficial. At least three guys from our neighborhood worked for the Oaks over the years as batboys: Frank Allesandro, Leroy Lawrence, and Howard Storm. Brothers Robert and Bill Young, Kenney Park regulars, went to work for the Oaks as groundskeepers to earn pocket money for school. Then, of course, yours truly, as clubhouse man.

The 1954 season was good for the Oaks and for me. Red Adams and I strengthened our working relationship. I did what I knew best and he kept the club in productive shape. I learned to appreciate personality, cultural, and age differences with a team that was greatly admired. Fortunately, there were no real prima donnas but we certainly had our share of curious and unique personalities. All pulled together to make the ballclub a winner. If it wasn't for San Diego and Hollywood the Oaks would have won the pennant that year.

My travels back and forth between Oaks Park and Seals Stadium—using public transportation—were dictated by the PCL schedule. Working on both sides of the Bay, I couldn't help but notice the spinning turnstiles. The Oaks drew a little over 200,000 in 1954, which was 70,000 more than during the previous year. The Seals attracted just under 300,000 fans, an increase of 125,000 from the year before. Both teams hoped the momentum would continue.

For a couple of weeks that summer, there was a Key System bus drivers' strike which forced me to rely on my creativity . . . the long and short of it is that I walked a lot. Whenever I could get a ride to San Francisco with Jim Moran and Bill Bradford, it felt like a luxury. With all of those part-time jobs, I should have been able to discipline myself and save some money. I was making enough to buy a used car, although I lacked driving experience and did not have a license. Whatever I could set aside for college, I did. That would all change after the new year.

Both teams ended up in the first division with Oakland one rung above the Seals. Red thanked me for helping him and though I didn't tell him, I was grateful that working for the Oaks had helped me abandon my long-held hostility toward the team. He asked me to come back next year preferably midseason if my schedule permitted; I said I would try to work it in even though I was hoping and planning to attend college out of the area. I convinced myself that it was great working for two winning ballclubs, a rare and remarkable achievement. So much for the rivalry; it only applied between the chalk lines.

12
Integrating through a Partly Open Door

In the winter of 1942, my parents and family moved from Third and Linden streets in West Oakland to Seventh Street and Channing Way in West Berkeley. My new neighborhood was made up of mostly blue-collar families from various ethnic, racial, or national backgrounds: Chinese, Germans, Irish, Italians, Mexicans, Negroes, Portuguese, and Scandinavians—all living side by side during World War II. There were two grocery stores—one block in each direction—owned and operated respectively by the Roccos and the Wongs. Two or three blocks up Channing Way there were two other grocery stores that belonged to the Soe family.

Around the corner from my house was the Firehouse, Engine Number 1, staffed with friendly firemen. The Bisbiglia Family lived directly behind us, while the Barajas family lived just across the street. The large mansion on the corner of Seventh and Channing belonged to Arthur and Edwina Troiel and their three children; the Troiels owned the metal fabricating shop where I worked part-time for several years.

The children at Columbus Elementary School (now the Rosa Parks School) reflected every ethnicity and racial group in our area. Located on Eighth Street and Bancroft Way in West Berkeley, it was one of three racially integrated grade schools out of twenty in the entire Berkeley public school system at that time. I like to believe that those of us who grew up in this environment were more tolerant and accepting of other kids, and that our experiences as children playing (and tussling) with one another had inadvertently prepared us for the future.

By contrast, racial integration did not finally arrive in the Pacific Coast League until the spring of 1948 (see the list of players at the end of this chapter). Following the lead of the Brooklyn Dodgers who had signed Jackie Robinson in 1946, the San Diego Padres signed catcher Johnny Ritchey who had played with the Chicago American Giants of the Negro National League. Ritchey had attended San Diego State College and made his mark on the varsity baseball team. His entrance in the PCL was hardly publicized in either the major newspapers or on that relatively new thing called television.

When I entered Burbank Junior High, I was stepping into an even more racially mixed environment than what I had known at my elementary school. I didn't give it much thought because I was still reeling from the fact that the Seals had lost the pennant to the Oaks on the last day of the season. Besides, after having spent several years at a fully integrated grammar school, most of us took the whole thing in stride and were far more

Johnny Ritchey, San Diego catcher

distracted by kids of the opposite sex than by their skin color.

Burbank and Willard junior high schools were the only two integrated junior high schools in Berkeley in the late 1940s; Garfield Junior High in northeast Berkeley was racially segregated. Berkeley's public school system was the first in America to establish junior high schools in 1912. The system was created by teachers who felt that it would be better to educate seventh through ninth graders (going through adolescence) in their own environment, separate from younger children and protected from older ones.

Burbank attracted kids of every ethnicity from the three feeder elementary schools: Columbus, Franklin, and Longfellow, all located in Berkeley's South and West neighborhoods. The experience of taking classes, playing in the gymnasium and on asphalt playgrounds, and being around all kinds of kids was a learning experience, and like most kids at that very awkward age, we had to learn how to get along with one another, no matter what.

Social life at Burbank, especially the awkward mingling of teenagers, increased our anxieties which many of us boys worked out in the gymnasium and on the field. I thought I was in great physical condition for a skinny kid. In the ninth grade, my height had settled at a whopping sixty-five inches and my weight, (on a good day) was 120, give or takes a pound or two. I had unruly hair that required frequent trimming and a face that I subjected to regular shaving. Somehow I convinced myself I was presentable and purposely immersed myself in a subdued confidence. After writing to Damon Miller, my level of confidence truly soared.

I followed the Oaks and Seals in my second year in junior high school by way of radio broadcasts, the sports pages in the newspapers, and sneaking into Oaks Park. By ninth grade, I knew that working for the Seals would be better than yelling, screaming, and suffering as a die-hard fan.

In 1948 Pacific Coast League baseball started to change before our eyes. It became more exciting when the Oaks started a new shortstop, Artie Wilson. He played brilliantly giving fans a brilliant twist of struck foul balls, infield chatter, authoritative hitting, and graceful fielding. During the second year of integration of the PCL, first baseman Luke Easter and third baseman Orestes Minoso joined Johnny Ritchey and for a very short period of time, shortstop Artie Wilson in San Diego. Wilson's contract had been canceled with Cleveland which pre-

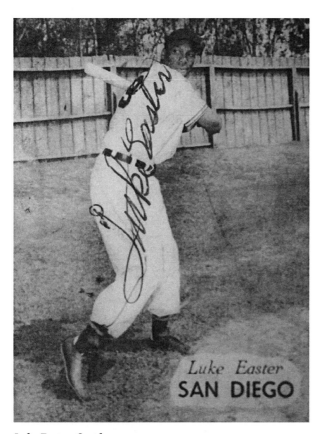

Luke Easter, first baseman

cipitated his relocation to the Oakland Oaks early in the season. His auspicious debut diversified the hotly contested tempo of the Bay Bridge rivalry. When I started with the Seals in March of 1951, I was so busy being elated to fully grasp the racial composition of the league. As Visitors' batboy, I began to notice a few Negro and Latino ballplayers, some native-born and some from Latin America. Due to their relative scarcity, they were fairly noticeable and had the spotlight on their performances. I met many of the pioneering players as they entered the partly opened door of organized baseball.

1951

During the major league exhibition games in mid-March, I had to wait until the Cleveland Indians came to town to catch my first glimpse of Negro ballplayers. They were conspicuously absent when the Pittsburgh Pirates, Chicago Cubs, and New York Yankees came to town. The Seals fielded Barney Serrel in the infield, Bob Thurman in the outfield, and Manny Perez on the mound. When manager Al Lopez brought the Indians to San Francisco, his lineup included infielder and outfielder Larry Doby, the man who was to integrate the American League; infielder Bobby Avila; first baseman and outfielder Luke Easter; pitcher Mike Garcia (pitcher Sad Sam Jones played part of the season in San Diego); and outfielders Orestes "Minnie" Minoso and Harry "Suitcase" Simpson. Like Branch Rickey in Brooklyn, Lopez enjoyed a sizable crowd of Negro and Spanish-speaking fans who filled the ball park. Owners of other clubs took notice of this potential market and followed suit over the decade.

When the Seals opened their 1951 home season a couple of weeks later, twenty-nine year old shortstop Frankie Austin and twenty-six year old outfielder Granny Gladstone came in with the Portland Lucky Beavers. Austin was from an established career in the Negro Leagues, while Gladstone began his career in the welcoming Mexican League, both were Panamanians. From my hunched position next to the on-deck circle, both players seemed to take the transition into the PCL in stride. The fans near the Visitors' dugout were positively receptive, which helped.

Controversial outfielder Jimmy Rivera brought his fiery Latin temperament with him when the Seattle Rainiers came to town. Rivera had been raised in the streets of New York City and had a fiercely competitive drive. At age twenty-nine, he was anything but dull to watch as I observed him

117

apparently lost in thoughts as he planned his next move. He came to town as if he feared nothing and nobody—similar to the way Ty Cobb played ball. Although we rarely spoke, I liked Jim and respected his moments of silent concentration. He could hit like crazy and run like a deer. The pitchers loved the day he left the PCL and went up to the major leagues where he belonged.

Shortstop Artie Wilson and "every position" Piper Davis heated up the rivalry between the Oaks and the Seals when they came across the Bay. Brick Laws and Paul Fagan took note of how many more fans of color came through the turnstiles. Wilson and Davis were not only good for their teams, but also for the box office. Each had his own unique method of taking a pitch to the body and handling retaliation. I admired their tenacity and resilience in the face of angry and frustrated pitchers.

At this time, the Los Angeles Angels' one Negro player was shortstop Gene Baker. Gene joined the PCL after three years with the Kansas City Monarchs of the Negro Leagues. At twenty-six, he was an accomplished ballplayer, good enough to be signed by the Chicago Cubs and sent to Los Angeles for seasoning. He was the smoothest fielding shortstop—and one of the better hitting—in the league. Watching him in the infield was, as they say, poetry in motion, and encouraged debates about who was the better shortstop: he or Roy Nicely. When he finally left the Angels, they were without minority representation for a time.

Gene Baker, shortstop

Alfonse (Al) Smith, the twenty-three year old outfielder from the Cleveland Buckeyes of the Negro American League caught the eye of Cleveland Indians' owner Bill Veeck. Long-ball-hitting Smith was signed to a contract and sent to San Diego during the '51 season. Twenty-six year old pitcher Sad Sam Jones (formerly of the Cleveland Buckeyes and the Homestead Grays of the Negro leagues) went to the San Diego Padres before Cleveland called both him and Smith back up. Jones was an imposing player, on his way to a long stay in the big leagues. Twenty-three year old shortstop and pitcher Jose Santiago came to San Diego by way of the Mexican and Negro Leagues where he had played for the New York Cubans. Before the Padres, he served his apprenticeship in organized baseball in the Colonial, Florida International, and Western leagues.

Sacramento acquired a gem when twenty-five year old first baseman Bob Boyd was signed by the Chicago White Sox and sent to the PCL. He had an illustrious career playing with the Memphis Red Sox of the Negro Leagues from 1947 till 1950. He loved Pacific Coast League pitching, even though the pitchers tried to unsettle him with knock-down pitches. Thirty-eight year old right-handed pitcher Jess Flores was born in Mexico and was in his thirteenth year in the PCL. After only ten games in the league, a thirty-nine year old Venezuelan—Alex Carresquel—had an opportunity to record one win against one loss.

There must have been over 300 players in eight ballparks for those 168 games of my first year in the PCL. Approximately fifteen of them were either Negro or Hispanic, an average of fewer than two players per club. The doors had begun to crack open but a fully-integrated sport and, for that matter, a fully-integrated America was years away. The Civil Rights Movement was in its nascent stages of articulating its aims, identifying its leaders, and organizing for its successes.

1952

By 1952, PCL team owners endeavored to open the door a little more. The in-group of players could see it coming. Old Satchel Paige was bringing the Negro All Stars to a number of cities throughout the country, including all the way to the West Coast. Many of his players were already playing in the majors and there were more who should have been. These barnstorming games were played after the end of the regular season in San Francisco, Oakland, and Los Angeles: they attracted a wide range of fans which gave evidence that the game's future lay in a more inclusive direction. After all, it benefited the box office and within a short period of time, strengthened the PCL.

The Seals opened their '52 season with the Portland Beavers and the return of Frankie Austin and Granny Gladstone. Manager Clay Hopper also brought southpaw Roy Welmaker, a thirty-six year old pitcher who had come through the Negro Leagues where he played for the Macon Black Peaches, the Atlanta Black Crackers, the Homestead Grays, and the Philadelphia Stars in the days before World War II. At the end of his career, PCL fans saw Welmaker pitch for Portland and the Hollywood Stars.

When Lefty O'Doul brought his Padres into San Francisco this year, he had with him a Mexican southpaw, Guillermo (Memo) Luna, who was anything but dull (and kind enough to give me a heads-up about Carlos Bernier). Lefty had also picked up right-hander Theolic Smith, a thirty-eight year old veteran after fifteen seasons in the Negro Leagues. The durable fellow could still throw assorted pitches with considerable skill. Somewhere near the end of the season, Cleveland sent down infielder Milt Smith fresh from the Philadelphia Stars of the Negro Leagues.

Tom Alston, a twenty-one year old first baseman who had played with the Greensboro, North Carolina Red Wings, had established a reputation as a hitter with slick fielding skills. He returned to San Diego for a second season in the PCL.

Following San Diego, the Sacramento Solons and manager Joe Gordon brought back pitcher Jess Flores and, later on, outfielder Pete Estrada. Len Attyd was a combination outfielder and infielder who had begun with Oakland before being traded to Sacramento where he played 144 games for the season.

The Seattle Rainiers were up next. They brought thirty-two year old shortstop Artie Wilson. Wilson's career had come by way of the Oaks and the New York Giants. He was still his old excitable self, keeping the infield charged up with steady chatter. He came back stronger and was hitting the ball better while continuing his effectiveness on the base paths, showing he still had a lot to contribute. Joining Artie on the infield was first baseman Bob Boyd who had arrived by way of Sacramento and before that the Chicago White Sox. They were two very dangerous players who could run, hit, and field as well as attract fans to the ball park. Manager Bill Sweeney also picked up pitcher Pete Hernandez from Hayward who pitched in only a few games during the season.

Manager Stan Hack and the Los Angeles Angels followed Seattle into Seals Stadium with shortstop Gene Baker returning for another season, playing nearly every game. For a long time, he was the only Negro player on the team and he was destined for a shot with the parent club, the Chicago Cubs.

Memo Luna was right. Manager Fred Haney of the Hollywood Stars came to town with none other than the explosive right-handed hitter and outfielder Carlos Bernier. Something like Jim Rivera, twenty-five year old Carlos had fire in his belly and played the game as hard as anybody I ever saw. He came to Hollywood through the Pirates organization and went crazy stealing bases at every opportunity. Like Rivera, he must have patterned himself after Ty Cobb because he made everybody mad at him, including the umpires. In a demented sort of way, he spiced up the game.

The last of the seven visiting teams to come to San Francisco for their first time in 1952 was Oakland Oaks. Manager Mel Ott had picked up a nineteen-year old local star straight out of Castlemont High in Oakland, right-handed pitcher Dave Mann. Dave could hit so well in the Oakland Athletic League that the Oaks used him in the outfield and at every opportunity against PCL pitching. Piper Davis was also back for another season, with thunder in his bat. He got knocked down a lot and knew precisely how to respond. The working agreement with the New York Giants meant that they sent catcher Rafael Noble from the New York Cubans of the Negro Leagues in 1949 to Oakland. He had played the '50 season with the Oaks, returned to New York for the '51 season, and then was back to Oakland in 1952. The thirty-three year old, right-handed catcher demonstrated that he could hit for distance. His contributions certainly helped the Oaks achieve their second-place finish.

After Barney Serrel and Manny Perez left the Seals, outfielder Bob Thurman and first baseman Herman "Lefty" Lewis were their minority players. Thurman had a pretty good year at the plate, could still hit the long ball and was on his way to the Cincinnati Reds in the National League where he would play for several more years. Twenty-three year old Lewis would play in twenty-five games.

At the end of the 1952 season, there were approximately eighteen Black and Latino ballplayers in the league, three more than in the previous year—not much improvement. It still meant that players of color comprised only eighteen players out of 300 in the PCL, an average of only two-plus players per team. Of course, some teams had more; others, none. I don't know whether or not the owners had a quota of how many minority players they would have on their teams, but it was clear that the presence of more Negro and Latin American ballplayers was challenging the status quo and that the players themselves were competing for the available slots on all eight PCL teams.

1953

The 1953 season "came in like gang-busters, but went out like we the people"—a popular expression in Negro neighborhoods. Bay Area sandlots exploded with outstanding Negro and Latino ballplayers who were anxious to make it into organized ball. Something dramatic was in the works. The big stars were players from the Negro Leagues whose performances had to be reckoned with as they made their way in the major leagues. Jackie Robinson, Willie Mays, Larry Doby, and Monte Irvin were all setting an example for kids in nearly every poor neighborhood in the country and abroad. The reverberations were felt all the way into the Pacific Coast League. It was now up to the owners.

In 1953 I had made the Berkeley High team along with a significant number of Negro classmates. Two led in almost every category before I even made the starting lineup: second baseman Carletus Gordon and outfielder-first baseman Earl Robinson. Both had major league written all over them and I supposed that there were major and minor league scouts following their progress.

Meanwhile back at Seals Stadium, the 1953 season opened without any players of color on the team. Sometime after July, two players joined the Seals: twenty-seven year old infielder Jose Perez and thirty-two year old right-handed pitcher Tony Ponce, both native born Mexicans from Ventura of the California League. Tony made a whirlwind entrance in the league losing to nobody and winning eight games. I was taken by the idea of two other Mexicans on the team and managed to have a few short conversations with Tony Ponce.

Manager Stan Hack and coach Jackie Warner brought their Los Angeles Angels and shortstop Gene Baker, who represented his race as the only Negro team member. Everyone wondered if the Cubs were going to make room for him next to or behind Ernie Banks, but Baker would have to wait for that opportunity.

Fearless, determined and productive Artie Wilson returned with the Rainiers, while Frankie Austin, Granville Gladstone, and pitcher Roy Welmaker came back with the Portland Beavers. Welmaker spent the first part of the season in Portland and the rest in Hollywood, winning more games than he lost.

The Oaks came to Seals Stadium bringing back Piper Davis who played nearly every position. Forty-year old Ray Dandridge—considered by many to be the finest third baseman ever to play in the Negro Leagues—joined the Oaks after playing a time with Sacramento. When the New York Giants signed Ray to a major league contract and sent him to the Minneapolis Millers, he became Willie Mays' teammate. Although up there in age for a ballplayer, Ray could still play well. Pitcher Jesse Flores followed Dandridge from Sacramento to help out Galan's struggling Oaks and Dave Mann came back for his second season finding it more difficult to get the hitters out.

Riding high in the standings, Bobby Bragan's Hollywood Stars came to Seals Stadium without my good buddy Carlos Bernier. He had made it to the Big Show with the Pittsburgh Pirates. Right-handed pitcher, thirty-four year old Latino Albert Osorio had joined the Stars after a time with the Louisville Buckeyes of the Negro American League.

On June 23rd, Sacramento arrived for their first of two seven-game series. Near mid-season they were deep in the second division, struggling to stay afloat. Catcher Johnny Ritchey came out of military service to spend most of the season catching and playing outfield. Returning for another season, thirty-three year old outfielder Pete Estrada played in only a few games.

When O'Doul's Padres came back they were trying to stay in the first division. Right-handed hitter Milt Smith managed to play third base and serve in the outfield for fifty-five games. Legendary right-handed pitcher Theolic Smith was in his second year with the Padres; approaching the ripe old age of thirty-nine, he was given another opportunity to help Lefty's club and pitched thirty-nine games, completing ten. Memo Luna was back but not yet ready to make it to the parent club, the Cleveland Indians. He went on to start in thirty-five games, tying with right-handed Bob Kerrigan as team leaders!

There were approximately seventeen minority players out of 275 players in this year's PCL, not much of a change from the prior year. The unspoken and unwritten word clearly pointed to a quota system.

1954

In early spring, the U.S. Supreme Court made its historic ruling in *Brown v. Board of Education.* The court held that America's practice of the "separate but equal" educational system in the public schools was unconstitutional.

America had a great distance to go if it was serious about equality. There had been slow progress in the area I knew best.

After the traditional exhibition games, the Seals hosted the Seattle Rainiers led by their new manager Jerry Priddy, an ex-major leaguer. Right-handed pitcher Pete Hernandez returned for another season and pitched more games. Shortstop Artie Wilson was now a fixture in the league and the fans loved his enthusiastic playing and versatile skill. I was able to spend some time with Artie in the clubhouse, where we chatted about nearly anything; he was easy with me and shared his experiences while he puffed on an expensive cigar and gave me the run-down on the game. He expressed concern about my progress in school and asked about my high school baseball team. There is no question but that he was one of my favorite ballplayers.

In late April, Bragan's Stars stormed in their first week-long series of the new season. Carlos Bernier had become one of my favorites by now, but I was still wary. Coming from a difficult season with last-place Pittsburgh, Bernier was happy to be back in the PCL where he could dominate the game. A local southpaw from the San Luis Obispo area, Don Corella, a Chumash indian, pitched in six games for manager Bragan. (I married his cousin Alicia Corella, from West Berkeley, seven years later.) Lino Donoso arrived from the New York Cubans of the Negro National League; he was a thirty-two year old Cuban southpaw who completed eight of the twenty-one games, winning nineteen with his good curve and blazing fast balls!

When Clay Hopper brought in his Portland Beavers, they had a new thirty-four year old southpaw pitcher by the name of Jehosie Heard. "Jay" had played for a long time in the Negro American League, pitching for the Birmingham Black Barons, the Houston Eagles, the Memphis Red Sox, and New Orleans. Pitcher Jess Flores, who had spent part of the season with the Oaks, joined Portland for the remainder. Both Frankie Austin and outfielder Granny Gladstone were settling into the league. In 1954, Frankie had his best year ever while Gladstone coasted. When they came into the Visitors Clubhouse, I made a point of not placing them next to each other. Some may have called that forced integration; I thought it was the right thing to do.

The following week, manager Charlie Dressen brought his super-competent and fighting Oaks to San Francisco. Dressen knew how to squeeze everything out of his talented players. He even looked like a manager, with jersey sleeves longer than his players' and a staccato walk when he wanted to get things done. Piper Davis had another stellar season hitting and fielding. For his second year with the club, right-handed pitcher Charlie Beamon played outfield because of his hitting ability. He started five games and finished one, showing that he still needed more seasoning.

Two weeks later, Sacramento—fighting to get out of second division—came to Seals Stadium. Manager DeSaultes had catcher Johnny Ritchey splitting the behind-the-plate duties with Bud Sheely, Ronnie King, and ex-Seal Roy Partee. Outfielder Pete Estrada returned for a couple of games.

Finally, O'Doul's Padres returned; they were an outstanding ball club full of guys having a good year. Third baseman Milt Smith was enjoying a good year at the plate and was considered a hot property; if the opening existed, the Cleveland Indians would consider bringing him up or trading him to another major league team. Big Luke Easter came down from Cleveland to remind PCL fans of his 1949 debut. At age forty, he could still send the ball screaming. Floyd Robinson, from Prescott, Arkansas, was O'Doul's pinch-hitter in three games. Back for another season, was forty year old Theolic Smith, who had pitched in twenty-four games to help the club to the pennant. It was Lefty's crowning moment and deservedly so.

Tommy Heath came close to taking the Seals to third place but had to settle for fourth. This was the year of our Kiddie Kar Express, so named by the addition of young players like twenty-four year old Panamanian outfielder Elias Osorio, and twenty-six year old Tommy Perez from Monterey, California. Right-handed pitching sensation Tony Ponce was back for another year to complete thirteen of thirty-two games; he won almost as many as he lost. Southpaw Adrian Zabala from Venezuela, age thirty-six, pitched his first PCL season after his arrival from Tommy Heath's former club, the Minneapolis Millers.

In terms of its efforts to diversify its clubs, the PCL did a little better this year. Nearly twenty-six Negro or Latino athletes played at sometime during the season. We were now up to almost three players per club.

Those who followed this first wave in the post-war PCL were eventually replaced by more aggressive athletes and ballplayers from vanguard high schools. Some of these were Charlie Beamon, Curt Flood, Joe Gaines, Jesse

Gonder, Frank Robinson, Vada Pinson, Willie Stargell, Earl Robinson, Pumpsie Green, and Joe Morgan. Each of the Negro and Hispanic players I met handled their entrance into the league in his own way. Like Jackie Robinson before them, many dealt with players who were hostile to integration. The weapon of choice was the "brush-back" or "bean ball." By knocking down the targeted player with a fast-ball head-high, you could express your displeasure. Sometimes if the un-welcomed athlete was a shortstop or second baseman, players who slid into a base would do so "spikes high," hoping to tear up the intended victim. The wall of segregation was coming down and with it the remnants of a "whites-only" cultural mentality. But, outside of the Seals Clubhouse, I had no idea how PCL players were being treated, before or after the games.

About to graduate from Berkeley High School, I had spent twelve years in integrated public school environments. Because of racial stereotypes, I wasn't always "typed" as Mexican. Yet, I still noticed how few of us there were in professional baseball. Baseball, as Ken Burns, the noted documentary filmmaker has indicated, became America's National Pastime. Although the progress of integration was slow, baseball and the PCL dramatically changed over the course of these and subsequent years.

List of Negro and Latino Ballplayers in the PCL, 1948-1957

Hank Aguirre	1957	San Diego	Lorenzo Cabrera	1951	Oakland
Tom Alston	1952	San Diego	Alex Carrasquel	1951	Sacramento
Luis Arroyo	1956	Hollywood	Bill Causion	1956	Hollywood
Frankie Austin	1949	Portland	Buzz Clarkson	1955	Los Angeles
Lenny Attyd	1952	Oakland, Sacramento	Sandy Conseguera	1957	Vancouver
			Don Corella[2]	1954	Hollywood
Gene Baker	1950	Los Angeles	Ray Dandridge	1953	Sacramento, Oakland
Bobby Balcena[1]	1955	Seattle			
Cuno Barragan	1957	Sacramento	Bennie Daniels	1957	Hollywood
Charlie Beamon	1954	Oakland	John Davis	1952	San Diego
Julio Becquer	1955	San Diego	Lorenzo "Piper" Davis	1951	Oakland
Carlos Bernier	1952	Hollywood			
Joe Black	1957	Seattle	Juan Delis	1957	Seattle
Bob Boyd	1951	Sacramento	Lino Donoso	1954	Hollywood
Marshall Bridges	1957	Sacramento	Solly Drake	1955	Los Angeles
			Charlie Drummond	1956	Vancouver

---

[1]   First known Filipino player in the Pacific Coast League.

[2]   Native American, Chumash Tribe.

Luke Easter	1949	San Diego
Manuel Echeveria	1950	San Diego
Pete Estrada	1952	Sacramento
Jess Flores	1939	Los Angeles
Granny Gladstone	1951	Portland
Jim "Mudcat" Grant	1957	San Diego
Elija Pumpsie Green	1957	San Francisco
Lenny Green	1957	Vancouver
Sam Hairston	1951	Sacramento
Bill Harrel	1957	San Diego
Jay Heard	1952	Portland
Pete Hernandez	1952	Seattle
Ted Herrera	1956	Vancouver
Tom Herrera	1953	San Diego
Dave Hoskins	1956	San Diego
Monte Irvin	1957	Los Angeles
Sam Jones	1951	San Diego
Joe Joshua	1954	Seattle
Brooks Lawrence	1955	Oakland
Herman "Lefty" Lewis	1952	San Francisco
Raul Lopez	1951	Oakland
Guillermo Luna	1952	San Diego
Dave Mann	1952	Oakland
Felix Mantilla	1956	Sacramento
Luis Marquez	1949	Portland
Walt McCoy	1950	Sacramento
Booker McDaniels	1949	Los Angeles
Ramon Mejias	1956	Hollywood
Pete Mesa	1956	San Diego
Orestes "Minnie" Minoso	1949	San Diego
Clem Moore	1956	San Diego
Tommy Munoz	1952	Oakland
Cholly Naranjo	1955	Hollywood
Rafael Noble	1950	Oakland
Lou Ortiz	1955	Seattle
Albert Osorio	1953	Hollywood
Elias Osorio	1954	San Francisco
Carlos Pasqual	1953	Seattle
Jim Peete	1956	San Diego
Art Pennington	1949	Portland
Jose Perez	1953	San Francisco
Mando Perez	1956	Vancouver
Manny Perez	1942	Hollywood
Tommy Perez	1954	San Francisco
Alonzo Perry	1949	Oakland
Tony Ponce	1953	San Francisco
Dave Pope	1957	San Diego
Bobby Prescott	1955	Hollywood
Wity Quintana	1956	Vancouver
Rudy Regalado	1957	San Diego
Xavier Rescigno	1946	Hollywood
Johnny Ritchey	1948	San Diego
Tony Rivas	1954	Oakland
Jimmy Rivera	1951	Seattle
Curt Roberts	1955	Hollywood
Floyd Robinson	1954	San Diego
Leo Rodriquez	1955	Hollywood
Roberto Sanchez	1955	Hollywood
Jose Santiago	1951	San Diego
Pat Scantlebury	1956	Seattle
Larry Segovia	1957	Vancouver
William "Barney" Serrel	1951	San Francisco
Harry "Suitcase" Simpson	1950	San Diego
Alfonse Smith	1951	San Diego
Milt Smith	1952	San Diego
Theolic Smith	1952	San Diego
R.C. Stevens	1955	Hollywood
Lonnie Summers	1952	San Diego
Joe Taylor	1955	Portland
Bob Thurman	1951	San Francisco
Rene Valdes	1956	Portland
Fred Valentine	1956	Vancouver
Roy Welmaker	1950	San Diego
Charlie White	1957	Vancouver
Marv Williams	1950	Sacramento
Maury Wills	1957	Seattle
Artie Wilson	1949	San Diego, Oakland
Bob Wilson	1954	Oakland
Parnell Woods	1949	Oakland
Adrian Zabala	1954	San Francisco

13

The City, My Clubhouse, and a '39 Plymouth

In the fall of 1954, I thought my life was changing direction as I headed south with Berkeley High classmate Bob Roth to begin college in San Luis Obispo. At the time, Cal Poly was a men's-only campus nestled in the beautiful inland area east of Morro Bay and north of Santa Barbara. The high waves of the Pacific Ocean that reached nearby Avila Beach just over the hills beckoned us on the weekends (much like the scene from "South Pacific" when Bloody Mary invites Lt. Joe Cable to Bali Ha'i). It was my intention to study Printing Engineering.

My loving mother wrote at least three letters a week and occasionally sent some money. Bob and I had a wonderful time attending classes, doing some homework, and checking out the locals. On Sundays we attended mass at the historic Mission San Luis Obispo constructed in 1772, four years before the signing of the Declaration of Independence.

By Christmas break, I received a written notice that my grades were unacceptable, effectively handing me an unconditional release. Bob was doing better. My schoolwork suffered for several reasons but the fact was that I was not college material. I returned to West Berkeley and the world of work, finding employment as an apprentice iron worker at Phoenix Iron Works in Oakland. Ray Hernandez of the Vocational Placement Department at Berkeley High

School had given me the job referral. Although it was good money, the work was hard and dangerous. I quit after two weeks.

I returned to working part-time for Mrs. Troiel, and with the money I earned there I bought my first car, a metallic green 1939 Plymouth with a jump seat in the back. It cost $40 from Patterson Motor Sales in West Berkeley. There were several dings on the body but otherwise it was a pretty nifty jalopy. I used whatever skills I didn't possess to drive a machine that required manual shifting. It took some doing but I began to figure the whole thing out, or so I thought. Because I insisted on "riding the clutch," I was tested three times before the State examiner reluctantly passed me.

A week before the March exhibition games, I made a trip into the city to revisit my childhood haunts. Until then, most of what I had seen in San Francisco was limited to car trips over the bridge that headed directly to 16th & Bryant. Now, I drove up 17th Street, crossed Market Street, and up the hill to Stanyan Street and Golden Gate Park. Over the years my parents took us to the beach, Fleishacker Zoo, and the homes of relatives. I had also visited the City with the West Berkeley YMCA and the Berkeley Recreation Department which took us on field trips to the beach, China Town, Coit Tower, Golden Gate Park, the museum and Hall of Natural Studies, and Play Land at the Beach. As I maneuvered my '39 Plymouth through the narrow park roads past familiar sights, I stopped and parked a block or two away from Fun Land. The raucous laughter of Laughing Sally—the large wooden female with a huge toothy grin—invited me back in.

Dick Larner, Jim Moran, Bill Bradford and Will Hafey had facilitated my commute to 16th & Bryant for so many years and I will always be grateful to them. I reflected on their generosity as I headed into San Francisco for my first day back at Seals Stadium. Standing in the shadows of the stadium behind home plate on Bryant Street was a local bakery's plant. Their employee parking lot bordered the west side of the incline that led up to the stadium's loading dock. The players and clubhouse staff parked their cars on the other side behind the Seals Clubhouse. Remembering that I was the new kid on the block, I parked instead just around the corner from Stanfel's Double Play on Florida Street. I stopped in and picked up a ham sandwich to go. Mr. Stanfel, the proprietor, wished me and the Seals good luck and encouraged me to come back when they served hot food. I downed a coke and headed for work.

One of the stadium's rolled-up metal front doors was open so I walked through and made the trek up to the concourse. My key to the Visitors Clubhouse still worked. I peaked in and sat down at the managers' cubicle and began to make some notes regarding the projected expenses of two weeks of exhibition games. Chico Norton walked in and welcomed me back. We talked about the coming season in light of the fact that the Little Corporation had only made a marginal profit the year before. As long as I took good care of the clubhouse and didn't start any fires, I would minimize expenditures. Then it was time to check in with Leo Hughes and Don Rode. They were in their eleventh and ninth years respectively with the Seals.

After getting updates, I returned to my locker room on the first-base side to get everything ready for the first of four major league ballclubs who would soon be coming to town. This was my first opportunity to work with several big league ballplayers and I looked forward to seeing the men I had read so much about.

I set up my General Store and secured the signs. During the '54 season I remembered a joke from the Berkeley High newspaper, the *Jacket*, and made a sign to be placed between the two urinals. It read, "I aim to please; you aim too, please." The other sign was a price list written out in an Old English calligraphy script I had copied from the moveable type fonts at my junior high and high school print shops. When I returned to the East Bay, I bought supplies at M and M Distributors and made sure I had plenty of printed check-off sheets to keep track of the purchases made by the visiting players.

Of the three or four major league clubs that came to Seals Stadium in mid-March, the one I remembered best was the championship Cleveland Indians managed by Al Lopez. The first guy to come into the clubhouse was their trainer Wally Bock, a husky fellow in his late thirties or early forties and generous with his compliments. He was interested in what I did, how I did it, and was charmed by the General Store. He even suggested the best way to make coffee in the aluminum coffee maker was slow and easy with the best grounds in San Francisco. He said Milo coffee is okay but "if you go downtown to the Crystal Palace, you'll find some other brands worth exploring." I told him I would. Then he asked me about the music and said some of the fellows might like it as long as it wasn't played too loudly. To put myself in a relaxed mood I had placed my new Magnavox portable radio-phonograph on an empty table in the trainer's area. My growing record collection now included Harry Belafonte's "Calypso," the Castillian's "Tango," and a Decca album featuring selections by Perry Como, Bing Crosby, the Ink Spots, and the Mills Brothers. I had spent probably too much time looking through the latest 33rpm record albums featured at the Sea of Records on 9th Street near Mission.

Manager Al Lopez walked in and introduced himself and immediately asked for a cup of coffee. While he shook my hand, he said, "Billy, you've got an awfully nice place here." He was followed by members of the team. Before long the place looked like Grand Central Station (I had only seen it in the movies). Harry Borba and Bob Stevens of the *San Francisco Examiner* and *Chronicle* came in to get interviews with the players.

Everybody I had read and heard about on this '54 American League championship team came into my clubhouse. First baseman Vic Wertz came in with a big grin on his face: he was the one who had hit that line-drive into deep center field at the Polo Grounds where Willie Mays made "the Catch." Larry Doby, the first member of his race to play in the American League, came in with pitchers Bob Lemon and Mike Garcia. Everybody, including second baseman Bobby Avila, outfielder Al Smith, and thirty-six year old Bob Feller arrived. The big right-handed pitcher said he wanted to test that glass backstop again, just to see if he could break it.

I wrote each player's name on the check-in list making certain not to forget anyone and added trainer Wally Bock's name. They were only playing two or three games at Seals Stadium depending on the weather. Then, they would head across the bay to play Lefty O'Doul's Oakland Oaks. (That's right; I said Lefty O'Doul and the Oakland Oaks. Wonder of wonders.) Before Cleveland left for Oaks Park, the team members paid their charges and clubhouse dues. Everybody was exceptionally generous including Wally Bock who added a twenty dollar bill saying, "You did a hellava good job for us, and I want you to know we appreciate it." I was flabbergasted: maybe this was the season's omen.

The '55 Seals resembled the previous year's fourth-place ballclub with some variations. Chuck Stevens and Wayne Belardi at first base; Jim Moran again anchored second base; Mike Baxes, Reno Cheso, Leo Righetti among others took turns at shortstop, while Baxes and Sal Taormina took turns at third base and the outfield.

Other outfielders included small but mighty Ted Beard, equally mighty Dave Melton and Bob DiPietro (at first base as well). The winter acquisitions and midseason trades brought in long-ball hitting and PCL favorites Walt Judnich who was from Portland and Clarence Maddern from San Diego. Catcher Johnny Ritchey came from Sacramento, joining Nini Tornay who was now in his seventh year with the ballclub.

Two Oaks pitchers crossed the bridge to work for Tommy Heath: Gene Bearden and Don Fracchia. They joined Bill Bradford, Ed Chandler, and Tony Ponce as the only regulars who were returning. Completing the staff were Steve Nagy and Jim Walsh. Tommy had wheeled and dealed to come up with a stronger team: the next six months would test his decisions.

The Seals opened the '55 season on the road with a seven-game series at Lane Field, the home of the San Diego Padres, then we hosted the Portland Beavers beginning with a Tuesday night game on April 12, the first of seven games for the week. I had enough time to accompany Shorty to the hardware store on Mission Street. On the way he points out the drugstore on the corner of Mission and 16th Streets and tells me that the coffee shop next store on 16th served good food; it sounded like good advice.

1955 SEALS

By the time the Beavers' duffel bags arrived, I was into my routine. Now in my fifth year in the league, I looked forward to renewing old friendships. Tip Berg, the trainer, was first to arrive; he gave me a hug and asked how things were going. When I told him about my first car, he cautioned me not to be a hot dog! "Showing off gets a lot of kids maimed or even worse." Then he wanted to know if I had bought any new records; I told him my collection was growing.

Manager Clay Hopper comes by with a big smile. In short order, the place is humming and I keep my ear peeled hoping to learn something new and interesting. They are talking about the movies downtown and I hear something about Glenn Ford and Sidney Poitier in *Blackboard Jungle* at the Loew's Warfield Theater. Local radio stations are playing Bill Haley's "Rock Around the Clock" from the film's soundtrack, "Melody of Love" by Billy Vaughn, and "Unchained Melody" by Al Hibbler. At the other end of the radio spectrum, "Jumpin" George at KDIA plays rhythm-and-blues standards featuring Little Richard, Fats Domino, and James Brown.

The younger players mention the movie, *Rebel Without a Cause* with James Dean, Sal Mineo, Jim Backus, and Natalie Wood, a film that my neighborhood friends Ronnie Lapham and Joe Swanson wanted us to see. As the clubhouse noise increases, somebody grabs my shoulder. I look up into the smiling face of shortstop Artie Wilson. He had left Seattle and come south to join returning infielders Frankie Austin, Eddie Basinski, and Don Eggert. We shook hands and I brought him a cup of coffee. First baseman Ed Mickelson, new to the league, came in; he had an impressive record for consistent hitting. Outfielders Luis Marquez and Joe Taylor, both considered power hitters, were also new to the team. Marquez noticed my phonograph and wanted to know if I had any Spanish music. I told him about the Tangos by the Castillians. When I played it for him later after the game, he moved about the locker room with plenty of verve in his steps. I wished I had known this guy when I was going to high school dances.

Big right-handed pitcher Bob Alexander taught me a fabulous card trick using all 52 cards of the deck while he told a story about 'a cab driver and a lonesome soldier.' As I watched him, I was mesmerized. He said "if you want to know how I do it he would show me sometime during the week." He wrote instructions down, step by step, and said he would test me when the Beavers returned. After the Sunday doubleheader, payday, most players talked about their next trip to San Francisco and the restaurants they wanted to go to.

Marquez suggested that I expand my music collection to reflect our heritage; I told him that I would. Tip Berg paid me and cautioned me to drive carefully and not to spend my money on foolish things. Pitcher Bob Hall, overhearing Tip's advice, reminded me to enjoy myself, sound words of wisdom from the big guy. I can do that.

The next day the duffel bags of the Hollywood Stars are dropped off. Because I had made time to go to the Sea of Records on Ninth Street and buy the 45 rpm recording of "Rock Around the Clock" I was able to create a jumping environment in the clubhouse. While I'm shining all those baseball shoes, I put the record on; from then on, I'm in a hopped-up mood. While it's true that "Music hath powers to soothe the savage beast," it can also make the beasts ready to pounce, and—for our purposes—dance.

All goes well for the Tuesday night game: the place is swept, mopped, cleaned and dusted. Both the General Store and the soft drink machine are ready for the converging athletes. I take a good shower, hot as I can take it because Lefty O'Doul says it's better for you and gets you relaxed enough to take a well-deserved nap. All is peaceful, and as the sun sinks slowly into the west, I am immersed in sleep. Deep, comfortable sleep. The overhead heater sends waves of warmth downward onto the clubhouse lockers and to the trainers' rubbing table. I'm out like a light. I borrow one of the Hollywood Stars heavy warm-up jackets and snuggle for what seems like an eternity. Somebody comes in very quietly and gingerly and walks over to me. The next thing I know something is tickling my nose. Half asleep, I think a spider or a fly thought I was a peaceful bony place to land so I snap to. Looking at me with that mischievous glare, blowing cigar smoke all around me is small but mighty Frankie Jacobs. He laughs and tells me to wake up as I'm in his domain. I jump off the table and he grabs my hand with his Charles Atlas strength which reduces me to a faint whimper. "Go make some coffee and make sure you put in enough coffee grounds, you useless punk!"

God, it's great to see him again. I follow his orders and meticulously put everything together. Before long, the pot is brewing Milo Coffee, strong as I hope he likes it. "You're getting better, but don't let that go to your head," he warns me. The players and manager Bobby Bragan saunter in and before long the clubhouse is absolute bedlam. I recognize many of last year's almost first-place contenders: happy-go-lucky Jack "Lucky" Lohrke, the dandy infielder-pitcher, and Lee Walls, homerun hitter and all-around good guy.

Maybe it was my heritage, but I found myself being especially moved by several of the Spanish-speaking Hollywood players. Pitchers Cholly Naranjo, Lino Donoso and impassioned outfielder Carlos Bernier seemed somehow to make my job easier and worthwhile. They seemed especially interested in getting to know me; my name Soto is a name from their own neighborhoods. When I put on my music, they gyrated and danced around in the clubhouse. Bobby Bragan didn't stop them and the other guys didn't discourage them. Dancing was one of those perks that I offered in my clubhouse, and the players were good dancers too: full of rhythm and enjoying themselves to the hilt. Carlos urged me to bring in Latin-style music, out of respect for our culture. I told him I would.

The Stars clobbered the Seals a couple of times in a week to remember, but the Seals fought back trying to make a decent showing. I took time making the sandwiches for the break during the Sunday doubleheader. When bill-paying time arrived, I was dealt with handsomely. Frankie Jacobs told me to get the lead out when they come back in July. He promised that things would get hot in the clubhouse then; Bernier said he would make my life miserable when he returned but paid his bill with extra consideration. Bobby Bragan said to keep doing what I was doing because the guys seemed more relaxed. I took that as a compliment.

With the extra money I made, I traded in my 1939 Plymouth for a 1948 Pontiac convertible: what a difference it made! When the Seals played the Oaks in Emeryville then traveled south for a weeklong series, I visited Oaks Park and talked to Red Adams about coming over to work their clubhouse. He said to show up in mid-June. In the meantime, I visited my roots in San Francisco's Mission District to learn more about where my family and I came from.

On Monday, May 8th I made it over the Bay Bridge by 9:30 in the morning and headed for the coffee shop that Shorty had told me was especially good. It was located behind the Mission Street Drug Store on 16th Street. I parked the car on Mission Street and walked around the corner into this tiny place with seating for no more than fifteen or twenty patrons. I sat at the corner and ordered ham and eggs. The place was almost full of working men and women drinking good coffee and eating good food. A jukebox in the corner was playing "Melody of Love" by Billy Vaughn so I thought I would scan the labels to see if there were any other tunes I might like. I randomly selected something I thought my older sister Lucy used to listen to, "Begin the Beguine," only this rendition was an instrumental piece performed by Artie Shaw and orchestra. The coffee was pleasantly strong as I put in a dime to play Shaw's rendition of the Cole Porter hit. I couldn't believe my ears. I loved it too much.

I read the *San Francisco Chronicle* and ordered the same breakfast, twice! After reading Bob Steven's piece on the Seals, I paid my bill and left the coffee shop contented and with some new thoughts about my record collection. I made it up 16th Street, found parking behind the Seals Clubhouse and walked briskly to the Visitors Clubhouse. I took my time getting ready for the early arrival of the bus carrying the Sacramento Solons and their bags. When it arrived, I moved everything, including the bag of bats, into the locker room, put on the soundtrack for "South Pacific," and went to work.

Around five o'clock there was loud knocking on the clubhouse door and the sound of a key working the lock. I jumped as Chico Norton was letting trainer Mike Chambers into the clubhouse. Skinny little me standing next to the robust Sacramento trainer, we looked like the long and short of it. We got reacquainted as he changed into his white pants and tee shirt. I didn't know how old he was but he could have competed with Charles Atlas, he was in such extraordinary physical condition. Looking at him made me realize that I could use a serious body-building course.

Chambers set up his trainer's table full of elixirs for minimizing pain. Manager Tony Freitas walked in with his coach, former catcher Vinnie Smith. It wasn't long until the place was jumping again. First baseman Nippy Jones and third baseman Harry Bright were both having a good year. Richie Myers came back as did Jerry Streeter and Al Heist. Donny Baich and Bud Sheely split the catching assignments and handled the interesting pitching staff. Chick Pieretti and Chet Johnson joined Johnny Briggs and Bud Daley, and someone I had not seen since 1951, Eddie Cereghino. Pete Milne, Jackie Tobin, and Tommy Glaviano patrolled the outfield along with others. The Solons were a struggling ballclub but Jess Flores was trying hard to get them into first division. Hard luck fellows who always managed to give the game everything they had to stay in the race.

Pitcher Johnny Briggs came into the clubhouse early during the week for a session with Mike Chambers. I was playing Mario Lanza's "The Student Prince." Before the Friday night game, Briggs walked into the clubhouse and handed me a 45 rpm recording of Enrico Caruso. On one side Caruso sings

Verdi's "Di Quella Pira" from "Il Trovatore" and Bizet's "La Fleur Que Tu M'avais Jette" from "Carmen." What a treasure, an old recording with such quality. I thanked him for this extraordinary gift.

The series went as expected: the Solons struggled with the Seals but managed to win several games. By Sunday they were in good spirits. When it was time to pay me, they were benevolent.

The Los Angeles Angels were to arrive on Tuesday, May 17. With not much time to spare, I prepared the clubhouse and purchased supplies, then went to see Don Rode. We talked about the good year first baseman-outfielder Bob DiPietro was having at the plate. They simply couldn't get him out. As I walked back to my clubhouse, I couldn't recall ever thanking Don and committed myself to doing so the next chance I had. Then, I turned my attention to getting everything ready for those high-flying thunderous Angels of Los Angeles. Midway between both clubhouses, I stopped in on Bill and Jack Cassidy in the concession department and got the Official Score Book which told me who the Angels were bringing to town. It looked like there would be a number of new faces, including one fellow the local press called King Kong; he was first baseman Steve Bilko.

Later, I made my way back to the Seals Clubhouse and acted as if I'd just dropped in to borrow some sugar from Don Rode. He wants to know what I'm talking about. I stumble a little but find it in myself to thank him for getting me the clubhouse job. He tells me that I'm a hard-working guy and deserved the opportunity. I spend a little time over there reacquainting myself with the ballclub. It was too early yet but they may be able to make it into the first division again. I ask him about the batboys; apparently they're all doing okay including Johnny McCormack and Mike Murphy.

After returning to the Visitors Clubhouse, and getting it ready, I took a brief nap awakened intermittently by the electric street cars on Bryant Street. Jackie Gleason's "Music for Lovers Only" played softly in the background. Joe Liscio walked in, smiling to beat the band, followed by manager Bill Sweeney and coach Jackie Warner: it was like old home week. Liscio said that I better have coffee ready since Sweeney was going to want some. I told him to give my pot fifteen minutes to which he retorted that they could wait as long as they were able to smell something other than the Pine Sol in the locker room. Hearing the romantic music, he wanted to know if I "had a broad hiding in one of the cubicles." Turning a slight shade of red, I tell him. "A broad in here?

I should be so lucky." When Joe reminded me to make myself scarce when the manager called for a meeting, I assured him that I knew the drill.

About this time there's a loud thud at the door and a number of the players come sauntering in, led by Bilko. The press had accurately described the new first baseman; he was big, with muscular arms and legs that were virtually the same in circumference. Other new players included second baseman Gene Mauch, shortstop Ed Winceniak, and third baseman Buzz Clarkson. No less than three new pitchers came with this group: Don Elston, Jim Brosnan and George Piktuzis. There were other new players who visited Seals Stadium that year. I found right-handed flame-thrower John Pyecha to be one of the most interesting. In the clubhouse, he was pensive yet seemed to enjoy himself around the other guys who were more gregarious. Sweeney held the reins on these guys; his team stepped onto the field, they were all business.

First baseman, longball-hitting Steve Bilko

Bilko did what he was supposed to do, hitting line drives everywhere. People stood to watch him during batting practice just to see him clobber the ball. Gene Mauch and outfielder Gale Wade played havoc on the bases. Mauch cleverly taunted the pitchers and timed it just right. Wade was just plain fast. The outfielders played a good defense in a ballpark that was quite different from their own with more territory to cover. Right-handed relief pitcher Turk Lown appeared where he could put out the fires. There was enough in this ballclub to give Sweeney a contender.

Tommy Heath had his hands full containing the Angels. Considering the batting strength of Steve Bilko, that's saying a lot. After the game on Wednesday, I took Joe Liscio to Berkeley to sample another style of Italian food at Granata's Pizzeria. I introduced him to Frank and his sister Connie and Joe felt quite at ease. After we ate, I took him for a short tour of Berkeley and the neighborhood I grew up in. Afterwards, I drove him back to his hotel—the Alexander Hamilton—in San Francisco then made the jaunt back home and called it a night. Before I knew it, the players were getting dressed after the Sunday doubleheader and saying goodbye. I felt satisfied that I had made their stay a pleasant experience.

Tommy and the Seals headed north to Portland for a seven-game series. During the previous weeks while the Seals were away, I had pitched batting practice to the varsity high school baseball team for coach George Wilson. Now, I mostly put in extra hours at my part-time jobs. This week, I picked up a load of ply-hole covers for Mrs. Troiel and unloaded them onto a table in the shop where I separated the defective covers, boxed them up, and labeled them for shipping. On Friday night, I went to a movie with the guys from the neighborhood and then to Hy's Drive-in on Telegraph Avenue in Oakland for a hamburger and a shake.

The PCL scheduled a Memorial Day doubleheader. Early Monday morning, May 30th, I made it back over to the ballpark to prepare for the team in first place, manager Fred Hutcheson's high-flying Seattle Rainiers. The eight-game series included a holiday afternoon doubleheader, a departure from the normal Monday day-off that usually allowed the stadium staff some down time; now they had to adjust their schedules. The fans came out to see the Rainiers play for several reasons. At least six ex-Seals were in the club: Larry Jansen, Ray Orteig, Leo Righetti, Elmer Singleton, Bob Swift, and Jerry Zuvela. The clubhouse seemed like one big family gathering. Only pitcher

Larry Jansen was unfamiliar even though he had pitched for the Seals in 1946 and afterwards for the New York Giants. Several newer fellows were also on the team.

I don't know where he came from but right-handed pitcher Ryne Duren could throw a baseball. Wearing glasses, he made the batters nervous and lose their competitive edge. Two guys that I could see eye-to-eye with were pitcher Vic Lombardi and outfielder Bobby Balcena. He was the first Filipino ballplayer, a novelty with the crowd and a heck of an athlete. Standing maybe 5'6", he could run, field, hit and play with heartfelt enthusiasm. First baseman Bill Glynn and catcher Joe Ginsberg were two other newcomers to the league; six weeks into the schedule, they proved their competitiveness. This team was loaded with good quality ballplayers who produced within the first two months of the season. Manager Fred Hutcheson had taken over the club with the intention of grabbing the pennant.

Trainer Carl Gunnarson was exceptional at his trade. Probably more than anyone else in the league, he was meticulous. We worked well together; while he kept the players in shape, I maintained a major league environment in the locker room. With the subtle strains of Jackie Gleason in the background and with maybe a couple of players arriving early, Carl and I enjoyed the music. We ended the week with the Seals getting clobbered by Seattle which pushed us nearer to the second division. The Rainiers left town on Sunday, June 5th, to be followed immediately by the Oakland Oaks and Lefty O'Doul.

I had been making it a point to get a head start on the clubs that came to San Francisco. Every Monday before the start of a seven-game series beginning on Tuesday night, I made it over to the city to be ahead of the game, so to speak. That's what I did on June 6 taking advantage of the time I was in the ballpark. Sometimes I hung around Chico Norton and picked up some pointers on keeping the place clean, other times I tried to find time with Don Rode just to stay in touch and get an inside view of the Seals. We were a little over two months into the season and they were having problems staying in the first division. Outfielder Bob DiPietro continued to hit the ball with consistency and looked unstoppable. They were also getting solid pitching from Gene Bearden with almost half the season gone.

I spent the week adding to my record collection with more Harry Belafonte and Mario Lanza's "A Kiss and Other Love Songs." A brilliant move since my love life no longer was. After graduation she went to Cal while I had a brief tour at Cal Poly and subsequently came home to work. As she would no doubt say, "C'est la vie." I discovered with great ease that life continues no matter the bad hops or strike outs. And so it did. To live it up I took in a movie at the Elmwood Theater on College Avenue, around the corner from the Berkeley Public Library where I worked as a page. It was *Les Diaboliques,* a French film with Simone Signoret, revealing and spellbinding. Accordingly, I was expanding my store of knowledge.

Bay Area fans arrived at Seals Stadium to support both teams. Lefty still had a loyal following in San Francisco, and the Oaks seemed like cousins. I saw Red Adams again, who asked me to start working in the Oaks clubhouse the next time the Seals went on the road. We agreed to terms with a simple handshake. There was no salary involved, just whatever I made in selling food, drinks, and tobacco, and clubhouse dues.

The new Oaks players interested me a great deal. There was outfielder and first baseman George Metkovich who told me how good the place looked. He had played with the Seals in the 1930s and had a working knowledge of Seals Stadium. He reminded me of movie star George Raft. Second baseman Billy Consolo and I got along well, in part because he thought I was Italian too. "Hey, Gumba! Que sidiche?" Outfielder Joe Brovia returned to the Bay Area after some time with the Cincinnati Reds. He was the same old Joe and could still hit the ball with gusto; he was obviously enjoying his reunion with O'Doul.

Players who were returning from the previous season included Johnny Jorgensen, shortstop Russ Rose, first baseman Jim Marshall, and catchers Lenny Neal and Art Cuitti. Among the returning pitchers were Allen Gettel, George Bamberger, big Chris Van Cuyk, and Don Ferrrarese. By now Jorgensen was a little subdued, but I enjoyed seeing him and sharing our conversations. Bamberger owned the Sport Chalet in Pleasant Hill where I had bought a beautiful snow sweater. Gettel was his old cowboy self; some of the players had taken to calling him "High Pockets" in reference to how he looked from behind. Lefty O'Doul and his coach Eddie Taylor had their hands full trying to get their ballclub into the first division. I was drawn to Red's goodness and his club's demeanor; at last I felt at home with the ballclub I initially disliked. My youthful loyalty to the Seals had clouded my judgment.

The Seals spent the next two weeks playing teams north and south: Hutcheson's Seattle Rainiers and Bill Sweeney's Los Angeles Angels. Around this time, Sweeney became seriously ill. Coach Jackie Warner and former manager Bob Scheffing had to take over. I returned to Oaks Park where I spent half of what was left of the season, while the other half of my time was spent at the Visitors Clubhouse in San Francisco. I had to let go of my job at Mrs. Troiel's until winter.

The Oaks had two more players that I had played against when I was at Berkeley High: outfielder-infielder Don Moitoza who came from Richmond High, and infielder Tony Rivas from San Lorenzo High. Along with Beamon and Broglio, they made me recognize the quality of ballplayers I had once played against. Since I was planning to play winter semi-pro ball for Johnny Valencia and the West Berkeley fellows for Guy's Drugs, I got in some infield practice during the Oaks batting practice sessions. Once in a while, pitcher Chris Van Cuyk ran me through those short hop maneuvers to help me improve my glove work.

The Oaks welcomed me back without an elaborate ceremony. Unlike last season when I relied on public transportation to get to the park, it was now the Pontiac and me. I found parking on the residential streets behind the first base bleachers. Fewer fans at the games worried owner Brick Laws, yet the ballclub plugged on as best as they could. Red made it sort of worthwhile with little things, like the eggs he brought from nearby Petaluma while O'Doul moved players in and out of the lineup as if trying to find the best combination.

After the Oaks finished two weeks at home, I high-tailed it on Monday, June 27th, to 16th & Bryant to meet the bus and the duffel bags of the San Diego Padres. I got ready to greet Bob Elliott's high-flying ballclub which was battling Seattle for first place. A week-long series opened on Tuesday night. I was busy listening to "Torero" when trainer Les Cook came into the clubhouse, approaching me as though I was the bull. It was good to see him again and in such high spirits. Cook was followed by manager Bob Elliott and coach Jimmie Reese. We enjoyed a few moments of relative quiet until the troops began to arrive.

By mid-season outfielder Earl Rapp was having another productive year at the plate, third baseman Milt Smith was racking up the hits, while shortstop Buddy Petersen, the hard-working hitter was going toe-to-toe with Earl Rapp. The hitters backed up the pitchers, specifically Eddie Erault and Jack Carmichael. But after the dust and Buddy Peterson had settled, it was the sluggers who kept the club in contention. Elliott and Reese had everybody hustling with outstanding defense from both the infield and the outfield.

After the July 3rd doubleheader, we had one of those rare gut-wrenching moments at Seals Stadium when Bobby DiPietro, carrying his best batting average ever of .371, hit a line drive to left field that ricocheted off the top of the twenty-foot wall. In the groove of continuous hustle he attempted to stretch the shot into a triple, sliding hard into third base. He hit the bag or the ground with such intensity that he broke or fractured one of his legs. The sound of the broken bone could be heard all the way up to the walkway high above the Visitors' dugout where I was standing. It was a terrible accident and costly to the club. DiPietro spent the rest of the season recuperating while the ballclub languished in the second division.

Bob DiPietro, first baseman/outfielder

By the time the Padres left town—not quickly enough for the Seals—they were riding high in the standings.

A number of episodes made 1955 a memorable year for me personally. Around late July, I received a couple of offers I couldn't refuse. Trainer Leo Hughes and Red Adams within a period of two weeks each asked me for a favor. Leo asked if I wanted a complete set of clean, traveling gray uniforms for either the semi-pro team I was playing with, or some other worthy cause. Red Adams followed with the same offer of a set of clean, home whites. I took both sets off their hands and approached one of the guys from West Berkeley, manager and infielder Rick Palfini who had a semi-pro ballclub up north. I offered either one of the sets to him, *gratis*. He opted for the Seals' traveling grays. I returned the other set to Red to be donated to the community.

The next unusual event took place when Hollywood came for their last trip to Seals Stadium that season. I will always remember Wednesday, July 12. Hollywood returned with what looked like a pennant winner. After the Wednesday game—and without Frankie Jacobs's approval—I gambled and played the Harry Belafonte "Calypso" album much to the delight of a trio of Latin American ballplayers: Carlos Bernier and pitchers Cholly Naranjo and Lino Donoso. The three danced to most of the album, entertaining their teammates and me, until the stern stoic look on trainer Frankie Jacobs' cigar-chomping face finally broke into the biggest of smiles. No one ever enjoyed my clubhouse music the way these three guys did. I wish someone had a camera.

The memorable season climaxed when manager Clay Hopper brought Portland to San Francisco the week of August 4th. After the Friday night game, pitcher Bob Alexander asked if we could have a talk in the back room. When we got there, he asked me to show him the card trick. I told him I had found time to practice it on my family and some of the guys in the neighbor-hood. I went through the trick reciting the story of the Lonesome Soldier and the Cab Driver. He gave me a few pointers, telling me to pause at certain points in the story as this would hold my audience's attention, but otherwise, he acknowledged that I had passed the examination.

The Seals' Kiddee Kar Express of '54 had been replaced with a streetcar full of frustrated hopefuls who could not get back into the first division and were six games behind fourth place Portland (Hollywood and Los Angeles tied for third place). The Little Corporation needed a better showing to convince the league of its financial potential. After the season, there was talk that this was the end for Damon Miller and his dreams. That was difficult to accept after I had heard Brick Laws of the Oaks announcing his plan to sell that team and move the franchise to Vancouver.

During the post-season exhibition games, Billy Martin brought in a team of major league All- Stars to Seals Stadium. I was somewhat surprised that he knew who I was even though we had grown up only six blocks away from each other on Seventh Street in West Berkeley. He scratched his head and looked at me square in the eye: "What the hell are you doing here?" Then he inquired about my brother Eddie who had been a member of Billy's Chinese Gang, a group of ruffians from West Berkeley who would beat up on other kids that Billy didn't like. They were busy all year around. He also asked about my sisters and my mother. I told him they were doing okay. With that, he waved at me and along with some of the players, headed down to the dugout and onto the field.

One month after the season ended, Don Rode, former Seals pitcher Butch Tierney, and myself got winter work toiling for the City of San Francisco's Department of Elections. We worked out of a warehouse on Broadway near Polk Street, setting the mechanisms for several hundred of the city's voting machines. There was just enough room to hit a tennis ball with a one-and-a-half thick ax handle. When we timed it just right, we sent the ball to the far reaches of this make-believe ballpark. Before the November election, we helped the Teamster truck drivers transport the machines to various locations throughout the city.

The *San Francisco Chronicle* suggested that the Seals might be lucky enough to find a new owner. Discussions were under way with a possible major league team. It seemed too far fetched to hang my hopes on.

14

Joe Mooney,
the Red Sox and Me

I continued to play semi-pro baseball during the fall and winter of 1955 for manager Johnny Valencia and the guys from Kenney Park. We were a collection of old-timers and kids. Among the older players were three teammates from Billy Martin's Berkeley High class: Ruben DeAlba, Howard Noble, and Babe Van Heuit. All three eventually signed professional contracts; Babe made it to the Cincinnati Reds. Others who had played with Billy at Kenney Park included Margarito Mejia, Ron Hartman, and Tony Sena. Other players included several teammates from Berkeley High: pitchers Manny Garcia and Joe Swanson. Second baseman LeRoy Lawrence was at least three years ahead of me in school and a former batboy with the Oakland Oaks. Another Berkeley High alumnus was first baseman Ronnie Lapham, on the team since we started in 1953. When he joined the military, he was replaced by one of the Valencia's teammates of old, Babe Vincent.

Like clock-work Johnny Valencia would send us a post card just before the weekend, letting us know the time, date, location and sometimes the name of the opposing teams. We played a lot of good ballclubs in Northern California including inmates from several state penitentiaries: Folsom, San Quentin, and Soledad (near Salinas). We played many of our games in the East Bay including all the parks in Oakland and at Washington Park in Alameda.

San Francisco

Official

SCORE BOOK

BAY AREA
BASEBALL CLUB

PRICE 10 CENTS

1956

With the Oakland Oaks gone and the demise of the Little Corporation, professional baseball in the Bay Area seemed bent on extinction. Then, at what seemed like the last minute, the Seals franchise housed in the Emerald Cathedral was rescued from the wrecking ball by Thomas Yawkey of the Boston Red Sox. Spurred on by the Sox's enthusiastic general manager Joe Cronin, the millionaire lumber baron Yawkey offered financial backing. The former PCL shortstop, Cronin from the Mission District, a member of the Hall of Fame, received encouragement from the league president. The other owners accepted the new assignment. If the major leagues were going to expand to the West Coast, the Red Sox knew that San Francisco would be a welcome addition to the American League. That was the plan, pure and simple.

While I was having a wonderful time playing semi-pro ball, Cronin put together an organization that would—in time—make it into the major leagues. He selected several people he had known in his "Roaring Twenties" playing days such as former Seals' outfielder Jerry Donovan, then PCL's secretary who now took on the role of the Seals' new president. Cronin wanted someone from San Francisco to serve as field manager and hired Eddie Joost, former infielder with both the Philadelphia Athletics and Mission Reds. Then, Cronin reached further back to secure none other than Walter "The Great" Mails, the pitching sensation and acclaimed showman who was hired to head up the public relations department. The administrative team was completed with Bob Freitas from the California League as business manager, and long-time Seals' employee Marie Snead, former usherette captain, who was hired as box office manager.

By early March, the stadium underwent a facelift. A new paint job gave it a sparkling bright look. The name on the front door read, "The San Francisco *Bay Area* Baseball Club." I returned to the first-base side of Seals Stadium. In keeping with past practices, the Visitors Clubhouse man assumed reemployment from one season to the next unless he was otherwise informed. There was no written contract and no salary . . . just an old-fashioned gentleman's agreement: a handshake and verbal assurances. It didn't surprise me that my clubhouse key still opened the door. It was all familiar as I walked up the concrete ramp.

As a creature of habit, my first action of the season was to get reacquainted with Don Rode and Doc Hughes. I opened the doors to the Seals Clubhouse, expecting to meet them only to be surprised by the unfamiliar yet friendly face of Joe Mooney, the new clubhouse man. He informed me that Don Rode no longer worked there. I started to worry if I was also to be replaced.

Joe told me to sit down and get acquainted. He said he was with the Red Sox organization and that their franchise in the American Association was the Louisville Colonels. Joe was interesting; he had the Irish gift of gab and the charm of a leprechaun. With dark wavy hair and a charismatic smile, he talked. He was a Yawkey loyalist and boastfully proud of his organization. He told me that things would be changing and that I should get ready to adapt to the new organization. (I assumed that this meant I still had a job and with an inward sigh of relief I continued to listen and observe.) Every square inch of the stadium would undergo a fresh coat of paint, inside and out. He meant the entire ballpark, and everything in it. I noticed the Seals uniforms hanging up in the lockers were now in the likeness and image of the Boston Red Sox, complete with color, style, and lettering. Even the lettering on the hats had been changed to match the parent organization's standard, although they still said SF. The thick heavy warm-up jackets had a picture of a Seal on it, replacing the navy blue Seals jacket with white letters across the left side of the chest spelling out, S E A L S.

Like Bob and Don Rode before him, Joe was another hard worker. He was a longtime student of baseball albeit with an East Coast emphasis. A native son of Scranton, Pennsylvania, his father was a coal-miner while his mother had worked in a local factory: a real blue collar kid, like me. I described my duties and he mentioned where I would work, so we strolled back to the Visitors Clubhouse. He thought the General Store sign was a little gaudy, but okay. He gave me the impression that we would work well with each other, and over the next six months, we sure did.

Business manager Bob Freitas and manager Eddie Joost made a surprise visit to the Visitors Clubhouse. They too asked me about my responsibilities, and then Eddie said to put me on the payroll. I didn't ask what my salary would be; whatever it was, it would be *in addition* to the clubhouse dues I took in, as well as the fees I collected on sales from my General Store. I didn't know what had motivated him to put me on salary, but knew that I had impressed them with the locker room's presentability.

Bob was probably in his late thirties, a slender tall man with glasses, short curly hair, and a flair for getting things done. He assured me that whatever I needed would be worked through Joe. I began to understand what it meant to be part of a major league organization. In prior years, I had avoided disturbing the front office personnel, mostly out of respect for how busy they were. In fact, the only time I had stepped inside the general office was when I first delivered my completed school work permit to Ruth Merrill, office manager. Now, I would be having a strong working relationship with the business manager.

Doc Hughes and Chico Norton were both excited about the stadium's makeover; the Red Sox planned to pour enough money into the organization to make the place suitable for its eventual transition into the American League. While it wasn't exactly Paul Fagan's original vision, it was beginning to look like it might come closer to it. The primary task, of course, was to build a team that could secure a first division spot. Much to my surprise, they would attempt to accomplish this with a group of mostly very young players with a few older veterans sprinkled in.

The new management would part from tradition to make their debut. When the club returned from spring training, they learned that major league exhibition games had been abandoned. When I walked into the Seals Clubhouse, I noticed the absence of many players who had been there during the previous season. Only three out of thirty from the 1955 team had been kept on: catcher Nini Tornay, infielder Bob DiPietro and outfielder Sal Taomina. I wondered where everyone else had gone.

The new team included some veterans from the Red Sox farm clubs, the parent team, and other teams. I observed them from the opposite side of the ballpark and depended on Joe Mooney's familiarity to learn about the newest players. The ballclub spent a week in San Francisco before the home opener, just enough time for me to get to know them.

I readied my clubhouse for the opener against Vancouver one week away then walked down the tunnel to the playing field. Local news photographers were taking pictures and interviewing new players. I looked on from the dugout's top step. Fielding balls at first base during batting practice, was little left-handed hitting outfielder Albie Pearson. When I walked over to introduce myself, I saw that we were a similar height and build. He carried himself as if he was over six feet tall. I had my glove so we tossed a few balls at each other. He laughed when I threw my floating knuckle ball and told me to keep practicing: "Don't let anybody discourage you from playing ball." I thanked him. As I watched the other players go through their fielding and batting practice, I noticed that most were not much older than me. I thought about the caliber of ballplayers in the PCL and wondered if these players could go toe-to-toe with them for the full six months.

They were impressive: young, enthusiastic, and determined. Ken Aspromonte was a twenty-four year old second baseman with five years of pro-ball under his belt that had been brought out from the shadows of Ebbetts Field in Brooklyn, New York. Another Italian from the same neighborhood as Aspromonte was first baseman Larry DiPippo, twenty-five, who also had five years in the game. Battling DiPippo for the first-base spot was twenty-eight year old Bob DiPietro back for his third year with the Seals after a '55 great year at the plate until he broke his ankle. Twenty-three year old Eddie Lavene had only three years in pro-ball but looked good hitting line drives and fielding

SAN FRANCISCO (SEALS) BAY AREA BASEBALL CLUB

Bottom Row: L to R—JOHN McCORMACK (Ball Boy); ED SADOWSKI, C; MARTY KEOUGH, O F; LARRY DiPIPPO, 1st B; BILL SLACK, P; BILL ABERNATHIE, P; NINA TORNAY, C; MIKE WARNOCK, (Bat Boy)
Second Row: L to R—JACK OSBORN, P; R. W. SMITH, P; ED LAVENE, Inf; KEN ASPROMONTE, 2nd B; GLENN WRIGHT, Coach; ED JOOST, 3rd B and

Mgr; JIM MAHONEY, S S; SAL TAORMINA, O F; BOB DiPIETRO, 1st B; TOM UMPHLETT, O F.
Top Row: L to R—MAX SURKONT, P; R. G. SMITH, P; JERRY CASALE, P; RUSS KEMMERER, P; BILL HENRY, P; JOE TANNER, Inf; TED BOWESFIELD, P; ELI GRBA, P; GORDON WINDHORN, O F; HAYWOOD SULLIVAN, C; DON LENHARDT, O F; LEO (Doc) HUGHES.

ground balls. Another young fellow from the East Coast was twenty-one year old shortstop Jim Mahoney with three years experience. He was six months older than I was at the time, six inches taller and strong; although he could hit the long ball, in Seals Stadium that didn't mean too much especially against crafty PCL pitchers.

Two other players—a catcher and pitcher—made me realize that Cronin wasn't kidding about making the team competitive. With five years in baseball, twenty-four year old Eddie Sadowski from the sandlots of Pittsburgh could hit, run, and do a great job behind the plate. The other fellow—right-handed flame-throwing pitcher Jerry Casale—was yet another Italian player from Brooklyn; he could hum the ball with authority and looked good in batting practice, too. Most of the other pitchers I saw that first week were young men. Time would tell if they could compete effectively in the coming six months.

Along with thirty-two year old Sal Taormina, now in his eighth year with the Seals, there were three other outfielders worth watching. From Southern California, twenty year old left-handed hitting sensation Albie Pearson had only three years in the profession. Coming directly from the Washington Senators of the American League, right-handed hitter Tommy Umphlett was anxious to secure a starting slot. With five years in the game, the twenty-four year old looked like one of Joost's starting regulars. The oldest player in the club was thirty-three year old Don Lenhardt, a right-handed hitting outfielder; beginning his eleventh year in baseball, he looked comfortably strong and capable of putting his experience in the major leagues to good use.

Much to my surprise, Joe didn't come to San Francisco alone. He introduced me to his wife Nancy who would be working as the nurse in the First-Aid Station. She was cordial, charming with her distinctive Irish accent. The three of us built a meaningful friendship on and off the field for their first season in the PCL.

The season opened on Tuesday afternoon, April 10. We hosted the brand new Vancouver Mounties, the former franchise of the Oakland Oaks. Local favorite and now the manager of the new club, Frank Lefty O'Doul, came home to rub it in. The press was eager to get Lefty's take on the new Seals and I listened as he described his Vancouver team and what they were capable of doing.

The Great Walter Mails came into the clubhouse to welcome his former pitching teammate O'Doul. I don't recall if the press was there but it was a moment worth capturing to see two pitchers from the 1927 second-place Seals giving each other a big hug and telling their endless stories. They talked about outfielder Smead Jolley who had hit 33 homeruns and batted .397. O'Doul had played the outfield, hitting the same number of homeruns but 'slumping' to .378! This all took place in the fabled, beloved Recreation Park at 15th and Valencia streets. As Walter left the clubhouse, O'Doul muttered, "That old coot could throw hard."

Vancouver's trainer Hal Younker had replaced my old friend and mentor (of sorts), Jesse "Red" Adams. I was happy to see Spider Jorgensen and George Bamberger as well, along with several other former Oaks. Pitchers Charlie Beamon, Fred Besana, and Chris Van Cuyk, along with catcher Lennie Neal and outfielder George Metkovich made the whole thing a surprisingly happy reunion. The party was complete when Frankie Austin (formerly with Portland) and Jimmy Westlake, one-time Seals favorite from the 1954 Kiddee Kar Express, arrived.

Of the newcomers first baseman Jim Pisoni stood out. The right-handed hitter had power, consistency, and versatility playing several positions. Jorgensen traded off at the hot corner with one of Baltimore's best prospects, Kal Segrist—young, strong, and destined for the big leagues. But the player with the brightest future was right-handed, fast-ball pitching Ryne Duren, a frightening sight on the mound. He wore a pair of thick eyeglasses and threw pitches that tested the skill of his catchers. Duren was all over the plate causing the hitters to remain loose when they had to face him.

The crowds came out for this short series, a seeming multitude that lumbered up the ramp and onto the concourse. They were noisy when they passed my doors. My curiosity got the better of me so I had to see for myself. It was a good sight for the new Seals front office as well. At the conclusion of the three-game series, Vancouver left San Francisco; everyone told me they looked forward to coming back in June and late August.

Celebrating the opening of the new season had to be curtailed as I prepared for the Portland Beavers who would come in for the only night game of the week, Friday the 13th of April, an ill omen possibly, and the weekend day games. Clay Hopper had left the Portland team to manage the Hollywood Stars and was replaced by former Boston Braves slugger Tommy Holmes. It was a sight for tired eyes to see my good friend Tip Berg again. He was one of the best trainers in the league and excelled at telling funny stories.

Portland was loaded with talented ballplayers. Returning for a second year in the league was one of my favorite players, outfielder-infielder Luis Marquez. From the Hollywood Stars came big Jim Baxes (Mike's older brother); he was a handsome Greek who looked striking in his white linen suits, making it difficult for the ladies not to stare at him. On the field, he could hit the long ball and was good with the glove. He seemed to be having a great time. Other Hollywood players on the team included outfielder Tommy Saffell and shortstop Dick Smith.

I renewed my friendship with Artie Wilson that Friday night after most of the guys had left. I enjoyed our conversations, him puffing on his cigar, me looking up from cleaning dirt off the spikes of the players' shoes. Artie appeared contented having been in the league since 1949. My other mentor and good friend was pitcher Bob Alexander who was back for another season with Portland.

Among Portland's newcomers was right-handed pitching sensation Rene Valdez, who mystified the hitters when he took to the mound. Second baseman and a favorite of Bay Area fans was the exceptional Eddie Basinski. He and Dick Young took turns at second base to give Tommy Holmes absolute security in the infield. Catchers Sam Calderone and Ron Bottler split the duties behind the plate. Overall, they were an improvement over the previous year's team.

Before leaving town Luis Marquez asked me to take him to several Puerto Rican markets along 24th Street. His bilingual skills were top level as I watched him get the most out of a purchase. Rice, beans and bananas, he called "Arroz con habichuelas y platenos." What had been an Italian-Irish neighborhood was now filled with the people and the flavors of south of the border and the Caribbean. Before our jaunt was over, Marquez bought me a non-alcoholic drink that was surprisingly good. I don't recall what he drank, but for what seemed like almost another hour we simply walked the neighborhood, nursing our liquid libation, eyeing the young ladies, and smiling at the older ones.

At the end of Sunday's doubleheader, Tip Berg, the players and coaches waited in single-file at my General Store to find out "what the damages were?" The process hadn't changed: I reviewed the tally sheet where each player marked his purchases, totaled it up in my head, and added $1.25 for clubhouse dues. They accepted my math skills and added a tip. Procedurally, it would begin when the manager or one of the players was ready to leave the clubhouse to get on the bus waiting outside of the lobby. I thanked them as we talked about their next trip to Seals Stadium. Portland would return twice more that season, during Memorial Day week and a four day series in August.

Afterwards, I gave Joe and Nancy Mooney a ride back to their apartment downtown. On the way, Joe suggested we try an Italian restaurant near Fisherman's Wharf. One of the players had told him about it and Joe and Nancy liked good food, as did I. He said it was near the corner of Bay and Powell Streets, up the street from Simmons Mattress Company. I found the place without much difficulty and parked as close as we could to San Remo's. This was an established Italian-style family dinner house. We went into the bar and introduced ourselves to the bartender, Nello Regghianti, who happened to also be the owner. We told him we worked for the San Francisco Seals and that was the "clincher." He said our money wasn't any good there, but we managed to make him think otherwise. After a number of drinks, we were seated in the old-fashioned dining room and for the next two or three hours we dined on French bread, minestrone soup, tossed green salad, pasta, veal, and plenty of everything.

The next morning, Monday, April 16, meant the bus bringing the Seattle Rainiers would be arriving at 16th & Bryant. I high-tailed it to the city, parked the Pontiac below the back wall under the Seals Clubhouse and checked in with Joe Mooney. I began to get my clubhouse ready for the next day's afternoon game and discovered I was low on supplies. I had to go to Oakland early the next morning or get there before they closed that afternoon. I went about the clubhouse listening to Harry Belafonte and remembering those dancing Hollywood amigos as I distributed and unpacked the thirty or so bags. When I was done hanging the uniforms up, I separated the clothes that required washing and drying. I still had to go to Oakland to replenish my store and then home to my parent's.

I was pleasantly surprised when I picked up the Official Score Book the next morning, reviewed the Seattle roster and noticed no fewer than six former members of the San Francisco Seals. Jimmy Moran had gone to Seattle after the Red Sox took over the franchise. Also on the roster was shortstop Leo Righetti, catcher Ray Orteig, pitchers Elmer Singleton, Don Fracchia, Larry Jansen and Lloyd Dickey. This was going to be a happy homecoming, to be sure.

Trainer Carl Gunnerson was first in the clubhouse the next morning. He was followed by the Rainiers' new manager, Hall of Famer Luke Sewell, formerly the manager of the Cincinnati Reds. Sewell was an interesting older man with an intense look in his eyes that suggested he was taking this new assignment seriously. He had the task of working with many players who had participated in winning the pennant during the previous year. This was almost the same ballclub that had nosed out the San Diego Padres and ended up on top of the heap.

Back for another season was the dynamic hitting and fielding sensation, outfielder Bobby Balcena, a friendly fellow who was easy to work with. Then, the many ex-Seals came into the clubhouse, starting with my old friend Jim Moran. They were joined by several new players, including Milt Smith from the Cleveland Indians and right-handed slugger Joe Taylor who played outfielder and catcher. Joe had been with the Chicago American Giants of the Negro National League where he earned a reputation for blasting the ball out of the park. If he gets one over the twenty-foot high left field wall of Seals Stadium, just 365 feet from home plate—that's if he pulls the ball—he will know he's arrived.

The Rainiers had plenty of players that made them the team to beat. Coming from Hollywood was Jack 'Lucky' Lorhke who could play infield, catch and pitch. He had as well the best of dispositions with a sense of humor that bordered on the hilarious while he was in the clubhouse. On the field Lorhke was all business, as was the former hero of the Boston Red Sox, infielder and outfielder Vern Stephens who had the look, attitude, and skills of a proud and polished ballplayer. This was also true of first baseman Bill Glynn and outfielder Art Schult; two weeks into the season, they were playing like winners.

Along with pitching ace Elmer Singleton, the Rainiers were blessed with effective right-handed hurlers, Bud Podbielan and Larry Jansen. Larry had led the PCL ten years earlier with an astounding 30 and 6 record, not likely to be equaled in our lifetime. Putting it all together, manager Sewell had another winning ballclub in Seattle. We had less than six months to find out.

The Rainiers left town on Thursday, followed by Joe Liscio, the Los Angeles Angels, and someone the players referred to as "Paul Bunyan." On Friday, I stopped in at Stanfel's for a sandwich and coffee and listened to the regulars at the bar talking about the Seals and how they should be doing better with all of those Red Sox rookies. Someone mentioned how young and exciting they were, but nothing like O'Doul's '46 Seals with Ferris Fain, Neill Sheridan, Roy Nicely and Larry Jansen. "I only wish Eddie Joost had Joe Brovia and Dino Restelli when they were the age of these kids." I asked for a refill on coffee. Like a fool who should have known better, I said, "You gotta give these kids a chance." Then somebody reminded me that it had been ten years since San Francisco had a pennant winner and that the major leagues were talking about moving West. I meekly reminded those patrons who were paying me any attention at all that the season was barely two weeks old. The conversation continued when old man Stanfel had this big grin on his face. As I was leaving to pay my bill, he leaned over to me and said, "Time's running out kid, the Oaks left town, the Little Corporation folded up, and we want a winner." Under my breath I said, "I'd see what I could do."

I did just that, I swept and mopped up the clubhouse, restocked the General Store, went down the corridor to Hirsch's Concession Department and made my purchases and then dropped by to see how Joe Mooney was doing. He was in good spirits as I told him about the conversation at the Double Play. He reminded me that it was the booze talking. The season is six months long, it's too early and you've got to give these kids a chance. Like I knew what I was talking about, I agreed. Bob Freitas came by and for what seemed like a half hour, we "shot the breeze." Afterwards, I made it back to pick up the multitude of duffel bags in the lobby.

I chose the inner sanctum of a silent clubhouse to reflect on what I had heard at the Double Play. It was nice and quiet with just the afternoon light coming through the opaque glass back windows. For the best of relaxing music, I put on Jackie Gleason's album, "Rebound," with all those haunting, sorrowful melodies. Before I could get into deep thought, Bob Freitas walked into the clubhouse and offered his hand in unpacking the bags. It was indeed a first to have someone from the front office pitch in and help me unload the bags. Before I could even thank him, Bob asked me how to hang up the uniforms. I gave him a demonstration on what goes where in the locker room, and piled the dirty clothes in the center before taking them to the clubhouse laundry. Before we hung up all the uniforms, we also had to make sure that one pair of shoes was placed on the continuous bench in front of each locker so that they could be shined. We were interrupted by Chico Norton who came in with a message for Bob. He jumped up, saying he was glad to know exactly what I did and how much he appreciated the chance to help. I thanked him and he rushed out to attend to his normal duties. Chico looked at me and said, "That's a boss and a half!" I agreed and finished the remainder of my routine before the Angels arrived.

By three o'clock I had time to shower and nap before the players came busting through the front doors. I put on Ravel's "Bolero" just to break the monotony. The more I explored it, the more I liked classical music. To make certain that I would have enough music to sustain my time in dreamland, I also put "Carmen" on the stack. Within a minute or so I was out like a light.

I was awakened by a loud knocking on the inside clubhouse door, the outside door was left unlocked for the arriving Angels. Joe Liscio, manager Bob Scheffing, and coach Jackie Warner came in wanting to know why it was so dark and who was I hiding? I couldn't avoid turning red which made them tease me even more. I wiped the sleep out of my eyes and focused on these old friends. Joe hugged me and said, "I'm taking you out to dinner tomorrow after the game." I said that I welcomed the invitation. Scheffing wanted coffee so I put together a fresh pot using MJB, my mother's brand. While it brewed, the rest of the troops trickled in including pitchers Johnny Briggs and Chick Pieretti. They grabbed me like I was nothing, forcing me to use what little strength I had to free myself. We all laughed. Johnny wanted to know if I had any new recordings by Mario Lanza.

Right-handed pitcher Marino "Chick" Pieretti

Suddenly, there was a loud pounding on the door, followed by yelling and screaming. In walked short-stop Gene Mauch, holding tight to first baseman Steve Bilko. Now, I understood what all the ballyhoo was about. Gale Wade, Bob Coats, and a number of players from last year's team arrived with more subdued laughter. This was a fun-loving group with more talent than was lawful. I felt it was safe to say they were going to be the team to beat. This was confirmed when I watched Bilko take batting practice. He put on a show of power, impressive even for Seals Stadium.

Effective hitting, good pitching, and snappy fielding make for a good ballclub. Even Joe Mooney was impressed, but being the loyalist he was, he never really conceded the Angels' quick start. After the game on Saturday, Joe Liscio and I headed for "Original Joe's" near Mason and Market streets. Smartly dressed waiters with impeccable *savoir faire* brought us our meal of red wine, French bread, incredible salad, and the spaghetti that Joe had ordered for us. After filling ourselves to our heart's content, I drove Joe back to the Alexander Hamilton Hotel and went home. I told my parents about the evening and promised to take them to North Beach for an Italian dinner they would not forget, but first I telephoned my Sunday sandwich order to Serge Ottino in order to pick it up early Sunday morning. Helped by good weather, the Seals and Angels drew a pretty good crowd for the Sunday doubleheader, close to 15,000.

For the next two weeks, the Seals were on the road to Seattle and Vancouver. I found the time to take my parents and Connie, my younger sister, to the New Tivoli, an Italian restaurant on Grant Street in San Francisco. I also filled in the time playing a semi-pro ballgame with Guy's Drugs at McConnell Field in East Oakland and helping Mrs. Troiel.

On Thursday, May 3rd, my routine at Seals Stadium resumed. We were to host Tommy Heath's Sacramento Solons and I needed to clean the place and get ready for their duffel bags. I was tempted to stop by the Double Play but in order to avoid getting into an argument, I opted for the small Greek diner across the street where there was good food and I wouldn't have to explain how the Seals were doing. Back at the clubhouse, I checked in with Joe Mooney to find out how his pregnant wife Nancy was doing and he assured me she was doing better. Everybody was doing better except the Seals.

Somewhere towards the end of the afternoon on Friday, Mike Chambers walked in. The very fit trainer for Sacramento was looking noticeably dapper. He asked how everything was going and I provided a brief report, brief because he had to set up for some pitchers who were in need of his magical skills. He enjoyed my Dixieland jazz. Pitcher Milo Candini came in, said hello and wanted to know how things were going since the Red Sox took over. I gave him my glowing assessment of the new ownership. The ballpark looked awfully sharp and he hoped they did good, but not at his expense. Later on Chet Johnson came in and wanted to know if I followed his advice and I told him, "To the letter." I can't remember what it was, and he didn't pursue it further.

Some players showed up as expected including first baseman Ferris Fain. I had heard and read so much about him. Three of their best players came in, first baseman Nippy Jones, outfielder Al Heist, and infielder Harry Bright. All had distinctive personalities, could hit the ball with authority, and were right-handed hitters. Heist was somewhat of a perfectionist in the outfield. Nippy was equally smooth with the glove at first base, while Harry was no slouch in the hot corner. Tommy had a first class team and he knew it, all they had to do was play their full potential and beat the opposition. This was not an easy task since across the league all teams seemed stronger than they had the previous seasons. Many had working agreements or affiliations with one of the sixteen major league teams. Sacramento had to depend on their pitchers to help out whatever the offense could muster.

Tommy Heath had no less than four former Seals on his ballclub, including pitcher Gene Bearden and outfielder Jackie Tobin. Other notable players included pitchers Joe Stanka, Roger Osenbaugh, and Bud Watkins. Watkins struck me as relaxed, full of confidence and ready to give Tommy his best shot on the mound. Given the overall strength of the seven other clubs, Sacramento had its work cut out. Yet, the Solons were a team with a lot of heart. I admired them for who they were and what they had accomplished with limited financing. Only a month into the season and they had hustle and enthusiasm. Tommy Heath must have motivated them something fierce, because they played like they were going to take the pennant.

After the doubleheader, Joe, Nancy and I returned to San Remo's and talked about the struggling Seals. For the most part, the rookies were over their heads, and the pitchers didn't seem to have anticipated the strength of the PCL versus the American Association. We agreed that manager Eddie Joost would have to ask the organization for some of their better prospects. In spite of our woes, we still managed to have a good time and the Mooney's were enjoying the cleanliness and the friendliness of San Francisco. After a couple of beers, I toasted them with, "Welcome to my home town." I was beginning to like the City more than I ever thought.

For the next week, the Seals went on the road again to Lane Field in San Diego and then to Wrigley Field in Los Angeles. In the shop across from where I lived, Mrs. Troiel put me back to work, packing plywood covers. She was a good employer and managed to give me enough odd jobs to keep my wallet healthy. I hadn't counted on how much money it would cost to drive a car.

The Seals came home for a short stay, a three-game series with the struggling Padres, now managed by Bob Elliott. The Padres were a collective of high-spirited players. It was easy now to see which teams were getting off to a good start and which teams were not. The Seals were struggling but so were the Padres. After finishing last year only three games behind the first-place Seattle Rainiers, the Padres were having trouble staying in the first division. Coach Jimmie Reese did what he was supposed to do and trainer Les Cook tried to keep the pitchers in shape, but the other teams were a little stronger.

Cook came into my clubhouse first, just like clock-work to set up for any players who required twisting, bending, and stretching. Always reliable outfielder Earl Rapp was doing his part as was outfielder Bob Usher; both men were hitting consistently. First baseman Dick Sisler was hitting better than ever. Outfield Floyd Robinson was also pulling his weight. Right-handed pitcher Pete Mesa was a newcomer to the league and looked good coming out of the starting gate. Ex-Seal Bob Greenwood and ex-Oak Al Gettel were helping out but probably not enough. They had a younger fellow, outfielder Rocky Colavito, who made you remember him. He hit one like a rocket blast that cleared the left-center field wall without any difficulty. Quick and loud.

The Seals left town after the Thursday afternoon game for a four-game series in Portland to be followed by a three-game series in Sacramento. They returned for a weekend series with the last of the seven visiting teams, the Hollywood Stars, to be followed by Portland's second trip to San Francisco. About this time the Boston Red Sox reached back into their farm system and grabbed two players destined for stardom: third baseman Frank Malzone and outfielder Marty Keough. The Seals needed the help badly.

Hollywood's new manager who was replacing Bobby Bragan was Portland's old favorite, Clay Hopper. Smart as a whip and dangerous, Hopper was victory bound with talented ballplayers. He came to Seals Stadium with Carlos Bernier and a kid destined for big things: second baseman Bill Mazeroski. The Pittsburgh Pirates sent them several hot properties that supposedly had a big future in front of them although they seemed secondary to me. Almost, but not completely . . . the exception was their trainer Frankie Jacobs.

Jacobs was worth getting up in the morning to go and see. He must have been in his sixties, but what spunk! He had more energy and unbelievable strength. When he looked at me, he reminded me to eat good food, cut down on hot dogs and Cokes, and lay-off that pizza—it's not healthy. He waited until I turned my back and then he'd grab me around the neck until I said the magic word: "Uncle." Carlos Bernier just looked at us and pointed his finger at me, as if he was saying, "I'm next." I tried to respond in Spanish, just to get him somewhat on my side, so I said something my mother used to say, "Uno momento." He just looked at me with piercing green eyes.

The teams were beginning to even out. Hollywood, for example, wasn't the same overwhelming ballclub because other major league teams had started to send prospects to other PCL affiliates. Their big first baseman, R. C. Stevens, returned for another season along with shortstop Dick Smith, infielder-outfielder Jim Baumer, catcher Bill Hall, and third baseman Gene Freese. Returning pitchers included the two other Latino dancers, pitchers Cholly Naranjo and Lino Donoso. Coming back to help on the mound were right-handers Ben Wade, Joe Trimble, and George O'Donnell.

Newcomer and "Bonus Baby" Paul Pettitt from the Pirates came in to get acquainted with the hard-throwing pitchers of the PCL, but it was Bill Maze-roski and R. C. Stevens who sent the ball yonder with regularity. Throw in the master of the stolen base, Carlos Bernier, and you have an idea as to the overall strength of the team, but it still wasn't enough.

Before leaving town, Carlos wanted to buy me a beer. I took him up on his offer and after cleaning and locking up the clubhouse, I walked with him to Stanfel's Double Play. Carlos wanted to talk to me and I obliged. I told him that I didn't like beer that much so he had the bartender fix me up with an Irish coffee with whip cream on top. There were a couple of other Hollywood players in there who kept a watchful eye on me.

I nursed my Irish coffee listening to him tell me that things were difficult for Latin American ballplayers and that I should be proud of my race. When I told him that I was born in St. Luke's Hospital on Army Street and lived in the Mission District, his eyes welled up. He asked me to take him there on the way back to the hotel. When I took him to where I had lived at 24th and Treat, we stared at the two-story narrow house. The expression on his face was well worth it. He knew the area from previous visits. Luis Marquez had mentioned to him that there were a couple of places to buy authentic Cuban and Puerto Rican food and asked if I would show these to him. We stopped on 24th Street near Alabama, walked a couple of blocks, and into this small market where he picked out something spicy and paid the owner. We talked about ourselves all the way back to the Alexander Hamilton Hotel. As he got out of the car, he turned to me and said something like, "Don't ever forget who you are. I give you a hard time because I know you can take it. Something else, I've played in the big leagues, very few of those clubhouse men have the heart that you do, so don't change a thing."

I knew then that I was one lucky fellow, that I could never thank Damon Miller enough and that I should take what Carlos Bernier was telling me and learn from it. When I went home, I told my mother what had happened. She just looked at me, didn't say anything, but must have thought about the neighborhood I visited and the unhappy memories it conjured up for her. I said very little else that night, just played some mellow music and went quietly to sleep.

Hollywood left the next day after the doubleheader. Clay Hopper came up to me and said he liked the way I treated his players and how well I handled myself especially when some of his boys razzed me for their own enjoyment. He handed me a $10 bill, telling me to keep the change. I was moved by his generosity, particularly because he rarely ate or drank anything and hadn't run up much of a bill. Then, Frankie Jacobs grabbed me and told me to "wise up," paying his bill along with a sizable tip. As he headed for the waiting bus, he advised me to "keep my nose clean." Carlos Bernier, R. C. Stevens, Paul Pettitt, and the rest single-filed it past my General Store to settle their accounts—I knew I would be seeing most of them again before the end of the season.

We were about one-third of the way through the season and the Seals' sixth-place showing was a great disappointment to say the least. It would be nearly impossible to reach the first division. Boston was learning the hard way that the caliber of the Pacific Coast League was only a fraction below that of the major leagues. The Red Sox organization would have to make some adjustments to survive.

By late June or early July, Eddie Joost was replaced by Joe Gordon, former major leaguer and one-time playing manager of Sacramento. Gordon had his hands full. Marty Keough, Eddie Sadowski, Ken Aspromonte, Hayward Sullivan, Gordie Windhorn, and Don Lenhardt had made the transition into the PCL successfully as did third baseman Frank Malzone during the brief time he was with the club.

Seals Stadium was no cracker-box, not an easy place to knock the ball out. People in Franklin Square and a service station attendant at the nearby Standard Station were still looking for one ball that had escaped over the scoreboard hit by none other than pitcher Jerry Casale. I heard it, saw it, and tried to follow its flight onto 16th Street, closer to Potrero Avenue. The arc of its flight was better than 450 feet away from plate!

Bob Freitas wouldn't let Joe Mooney and I lick our wounds. Instead, he gave us an assignment to play stadium watchmen during the winter months. We helped Harvey and Shorty place all the movable box seats in the stadium concourse out of the way of winter rain. We moved into the usherette's quarters—many years before it had served as the clubhouse for the Mission Reds. There we cooked, ate, and cleaned up after ourselves and kept our eye on Seals Stadium. Joe got additional part-time work as a fireman on the Southern Pacific Railways while I landed a full-time job at Simmons Mattress Company near San Remo's, where I made good money as a coil springs assembler. It was piece work, which meant you worked as fast as you could: the more you made, the more you got paid.

Nancy Mooney returned to Scranton to have her baby. Eventually, Joe joined her. My relationship with the Red Sox organization had firmly established itself and grew steadily. They knew how to take care of their hired hands. That winter of 1956 was Boston's maiden voyage through the Golden Gate. Major improvements would be necessary if the franchise was to be added to the American League. Tom Yawkey, Joe Cronin, Jerry Donovan, and Joe Gordon would spend the winter making whatever changes they needed to translate into a more acceptable placement in the standings.

15

Major League,
Our Time Has Come

Working in North Beach gave me easy access to the best Italian family markets that specialized in sandwiches for the workers in the surrounding area. I was one of them, employed on the second floor of the Simmons Mattress Factory, assembling coil springs. I didn't know my hands could work so fast.

I worked with a cadre of younger fellows. One of them was Jésus De Jésus, a Puerto Rican who was short like me, and looked like an ex-fighter. We talked as we assembled the coil springs, making relatively good money doing piecework. The down side was that once-in-a-while a less enthusiastic worker would "borrow" one of your tickets that determined your pay.

Joe Mooney had returned to Scranton to be with his family and I was left to my own devices. I had to vacate the usherette's domain at Seals Stadium and return to my parent's home in West Berkeley. I was burning the candle at both ends and succumbed to a severe case of bronchial asthma. Under a doctor's care, who treated me with medication and sound advice to slow down, I recovered.

In early 1957, I received notice from the Selective Service to report for my physical examination. I did so, taking along a letter from Dr. Kozar who confirmed that I had recently been cured of asthma and was in good health. Like a good citizen, I gave the letter to the Selective Service and took their exam. I had also registered as a Democrat and began to read the newspapers with greater interest, figuring that if I was going to serve my country I should know something about it.

I was twenty-one and had never taken life too seriously. I worked, played ball, generally stayed out of trouble and kept unusual hours. My mother was hoping for my induction; I think she thought that I needed the discipline, but after a couple of weeks, the Selective Service sent me a letter exempting me from the draft.

February turned to March. The Seals came back to the Stadium and I returned to the life I most enjoyed. About this time, I traded my '48 Pontiac for a cream-green 1950 Oldsmobile, complete with a white and Kelly-green Naugahyde interior and a pretty good engine. I found it on the lot of a car dealer along auto row on Broadway Street in Oakland. When I drove to San Francisco, it felt like I was crossing the bridge in style. On my way over, I couldn't help but notice the Key System's trains running back and forth on the bottom deck of the bridge and remembered what it used to be like.

I felt that this was going to be a better year working for the Boston Red Sox. I read the *Chronicle's* coverage of the deals that had been made over the winter. Jerry Donovan and Joe Gordon were given the funds to produce a better ballclub in the highly competitive PCL. Some of Boston's best young players and a few veterans could get the ballclub to where they hadn't been in three years—the first division. Soon, I would have the straight scoop from Irish Joe Mooney.

I parked out of the way of delivery trucks and walked into the Seals Clubhouse to meet Joe Mooney, the new father. He offered me a cigar with a pink band around it. I asked him how Nancy and his new daughter Jo Ann were doing and he assured me that everything was okay. We talked about the new season and the upcoming mid-March weekend exhibition games with the parent club. He wouldn't say too much other than "Let's just wait and see." Leo Hughes seemed enthusiastic having had the opportunity to work with the new team at the training facilities in Fullerton.

With only a week until the three-game weekend series with the Red Sox, there was plenty to do. I swept and scrubbed the place, giving special attention to the wooden shower floor mats, the toilets and urinals. Chico Norton, who did a "white glove inspection" when I was through, was pleased.

From Wednesday on, I went down to the field to check out the new players. Southpaw Leo Kiley was back for his second season as were right-handed Bill Abernathie and left-hander Bob Smith who competed for the starting spots with ex-major leaguers Jim Konstanty, the forty year old, right-hander from the Yankees; Walter Masterson, the almost thirty-six year old right-hander from Detroit; Harry Dorish, the thirty-four year old right-hander from Boston; and Duane Pillete, the almost thirty-four year old right-hander from the Phillies. As younger players, Kiley, Abernathie, and Smith gave manager Joe Gordon a more balanced pitching staff. The only one of the six I had ever worked with before was Pillete; he had been with the '55 Oaks.

Of the outfielders, dependable, reliable Sal Taormina returned for another season along with Bob DiPietro, Tommy Umphlett, Marty Keough, and Albie Pearson. Joining them were newcomers Hal Grote from Birmingham of the Southern Association and Bill Renna from Richmond of the International League. The returning infielders were second baseman Ken Aspromonte and third baseman Joe Tanner. Harry Malmberg, the thirty-one year old shortstop from Charleston of the American Association was another newcomer, along with thirty-four old infielder and pitcher Grady Hatton, from the St. Louis Cardinals and thirty-three year old Frank Kellert from the Chicago Cubs. That left the catching assignments to Nini Tornay, now in his ninth year with the Seals, and Eddie Sadowski, one of two prospects being groomed for the parent club. Overall, manager Joe Gordon, coach Glenn Wright and trainer Leo Hughes would be working with mostly experienced players.

As the season got underway, there was some fine tuning and a trade or two, but mostly this was a ballclub worth watching. Before they took on the seven other clubs in the league, they had to face Ted Williams and the Boston Red Sox. It sounds like one of those science fiction monster movies that is worth canceling all other activities in order to see. I told Joe Mooney and Bob Freitas that even though I was working for the other side, my heart was hinged to the ballclub that had hired me into my seventh season. I hoped that the '7' meant good luck.

I was jittery as the Red Sox arrived for the series on Thursday, March 21st. In the late afternoon, their bus pulled into the front lobby and I scurried to unload the bags. The 1957 routine began the way every season since 1954 had begun. Mooney came by to make sure everything was there, probably on the advice of management or the Red Sox trainer. Once in the clubhouse, we threw the bags in every direction, placing Jimmy Piersall and Ted Williams near the end lockers, just under the ceiling heater. I completed the process as Joe headed back to his side of the stadium.

Satisfied we were ready for our parent club, I put on Frank Sinatra and was quickly lulled to sleep; later Chico woke me up and I headed home. The next morning, I aimed my Olds back to the City, stopping at the Greek coffee shop, and then headed to the clubhouse to double-check my preparations. As I washed out the coffee pot, a piece of the equipment fell apart; I had to make a quick decision: either buy coffee from the concession stand or go out and get a new coffee pot. Cleveland trainer Wally Bock had once told me about the various brands of coffees and coffee makers at the Crystal Palace on Market Street. I thought, "I've got time" so I locked up and let Mooney know where I was going. It was about 10:30 as I headed downtown. Easy parking, I took my time finding the place and watching all the people in San Francisco's busy central shopping district.

I was in a good mood, anticipating the crowd and their excitement over the Red Sox. The clerk showed me several kinds of coffee makers and just as I began to make my selection, I heard a loud roar as if a jet plane had broken through the sound barrier. The building made a weird creaking noise, as if it was being stretched. The shelves began to rattle and an elderly man yelled out, "It's a quake." We all headed for the front doors.

It was a quake all right, one with sharp jolts followed by a sequence of lighter shocks. The overhead lights in the store swung back and forth as people milled about on the sidewalk in front of the store and down the block. After a while, we headed back into the shops; I found what I was looking for and returned to the comfort of 16th & Bryant. There, I found Mooney all excited as he, Chico, and the groundskeepers walked through the stadium to assess the damage. According to them, hardly anything was noticeable.

There were several aftershocks throughout the afternoon. Stanfel's place was full of men and a few women who were sipping whatever they needed to calm their nerves. I ordered a sandwich and headed back to the ballpark. The marquee announced that the Red Sox and the Seals would be locking horns at 8 p.m.

This is what it must have been like on my first day at work seven years back. The Bay Area was getting ready to welcome another major league team to San Francisco. Bill and Jack Cassidy opened the concession department; Joe Mooney and I picked up our beverages and two sacks of ice. I copied the names from the Official Score Book onto my list and waited in the clubhouse for the players to arrive. There were a few more light aftershocks and I decided not to take a nap. I did not want to be awakened from a deep sleep in order to greet the new parent organization. No, not at all.

Around 4:30 in the afternoon, a number of hometown players made it to Mooney's clubhouse and were discussing the quake. For some players, it was their first experience of an earthquake, but for Bob DiPietro, Sal Taormina, and Nini Tornay, it was familiar territory. I got back to my side of the stadium a half hour before the Red Sox trainer arrived, unnerved by the aftershocks but easily reassured by a cup of coffee. He was followed by the rest of the ballclub in no particular order. Everyone located their lockers and there was a lot of chatter as the players anxiously awaited the game.

As with all the major league clubs that had preceded these ballplayers into Seals Stadium, there was a mixture of rookies and veterans. Two stood out by the end of the evening. Pinky Higgins was their rather unexcitable manager. Dick Dobbins, a familiar face from Berkeley High School, entered with a camera in his hands. I checked with the trainer who let Dick take several shots of Ted Williams; forty-two years later the photograph appeared in Dobbin's book *A Grand Minor League*. After Dick left, I checked on the crowd and was flabbergasted to see so many fans coming up the ramp.

Outfielder Jimmy Piersall spent most of the game in the clubhouse, first on the trainer's table and then sitting in his locker having a cup of coffee with me. He talked openly about his men-

Berkeley High School classmate Dick Dobbins with Ted Williams

tal breakdown and the movie *Fear Strikes Out,* that had been made about him. His first choice to play his character had been James Dean, but that actor's untimely death resulted in Anthony Perkins carrying the part. Jimmy asked about my ambitions and he suggested that I have alternate plans in the event of any unforeseen circumstances. It sounded like good advice at the time. I rarely got an opportunity to go one-on-one with a major leaguer and when I did, I was a good listener.

After the game, the players showered, changed, and left for the hotel—everyone that is except for Ted Williams who stayed to chat with Jimmy about hunting and fishing. As he searched through his duffel bag, he couldn't locate his shaving gear and asked to borrow mine. At last the two players left and I cleaned up, calling to let Mooney know that I would be sleeping over in the clubhouse. He told me that Bob Freitas also wanted to stay overnight rather than take the train back to San Jose, so Bob and I talked ourselves to sleep on the carpeted floor of the Ladies Lounge.

The weekend came to a halt after the Sunday game which had attracted the best attendance ever at Seals Stadium for a three-game series: over 60,000 fans! I do not recall the final scores of all three games, but I know the fans were treated to an event of significant proportion. It was a glimpse into the future of Bay Area baseball, with the Seals and the Red Sox in the American League! I couldn't wait for the historic day.

The PCL returned to the popular week-long seven-game series. Joe Gordon opened the '57 season on Thursday afternoon, April 11, with another one of my favorite managers, Bill Sweeney who had brought his Portland players for a season opener. I had the chance to work again with trainer Tip Berg.

Joe Gordon, manager

170

By this time, we knew each other's routines well. I did my stuff and listened to his wonderful tales.

Luis Marquez came back for another season, having had an outstanding year at the plate the previous year. It seems that hitting .344 should have given him a shot at the majors, but Luis didn't make it. First baseman Ed Mickelson returned after a season hitting over .300. Perennial favorite second baseman Eddie Basinski came back, too, for his eleventh season with Portland. Infielder Artie Wilson was traded to Sacramento, replaced by newcomer Eddie Winceniak, a personable young man who was easy to work for.

Sweeney's pitching staff saw the return of right-hander Bob Alexander who kept me on top of my card tricks. He also tried to teach me how to guess the correct change in somebody's pockets, but I struggled to catch on to this new trick. There were several newcomers who had joined the club, including outfielder Solly Drake, a switch-hitting outfielder who could run like a deer. Pitchers Johnny Briggs and Dave Hillman, as well as infielders Casey Wise and George Freese had come over from the Los Angeles Angels, a team that had won last year's pennant. Their presence was going to give Portland an opportunity to make it into the first division, although it was too soon to tell.

This was a fun-loving group who had come together at a time when most clubs in the league had direct working agreements or affiliations with a major league ballclub. While they were in the clubhouse, they loved to talk about good local eateries: Tommy's Joint on Van Ness, Original Joe's at the foot of Mason Street. Somebody mentioned Rathskellar's on Polk Street as a great place for German food, and Ernie's on Broadway for Italian cuisine. I told them about San Remo's and the New Tivoli.

Portland had a difficult week with the new Seals who came out of the gate swinging for the fences. Sweeney's guys were fierce competitors and they made the contests exciting. The Seals were ready to avenge last year's poor showing.

With a half day off, I returned to the ballpark again on Monday morning in time to gather up the Seattle Rainiers' duffel bags. All the local papers carried a feature about their new manager, and the City's favorite son, Lefty O'Doul, a true embodiment of the saying that "You can't keep a good man down." After he had landed in last place with Vancouver, Lefty could only rise in the standings now.

The marquee on 16th Street proclaimed an 8:15 p.m. game on Tuesday, April 16. Since Lefty and his boys would arrive around 5:30, I had to hustle to get the clubhouse ready but by now, my routine was set to guarantee that the Visitors would be well treated.

Trainer Freddie Frederico, who replaced Carol Gunnerson, was the first to arrive. Everybody headed back to the trainer's table where Freddie worked his magical powers. He would twist and stretch the arms and legs of southpaw relief pitcher Bill Kennedy and starter Marion Fricano to perfection. By now, my coffee was going and the General Store was open for business. I went outside to see if any visiting players were perched near the top row of the box seats, watching the Seals take batting practice. Then Lefty showed up with his new coach, Edo Vanni, signaling it was time for everyone to get inside.

Outfielder Bobby Balcena and trainer Fredricco acquainted the newer players to the clubhouse procedures. For me, a ballclub's first trip to San Francisco was an opportunity to learn something about the people I would be working with. I first took notice of the infielders since I fancied myself one (at the time, I was in my fourth season of semi-pro ball as the starting shortstop with Guy's Drugs). Maury Wills was filling the shortstop position for the Rainiers, which had been vacated by Leo Righetti who had gone to Sacramento. Several new fellows replaced Bill Glynn at first base; Glynn had held the job for two seasons. Now, right-handed Hal Bevan alternated with Jimmy Dyck and others. There were a number of new players who took turns at the hot corner vacated by Milt Smith. Lefty pulled players in and out from several positions to find the right mix, sometimes using newcomer Juan Delis at third base and in the outfield, taking advantage of the right-handed hitter's abilities.

Lefty's outfield included hustling Bobby Balcena back for a third season and bringing back the homerun hitting Joe Taylor for a second year. Catchers Ray Orteig and Dick Aylward handled the pitching with expertise. Their battery mates were a stable of veterans and younger fellows. Southpaw Charlie Rabe and Lefty Haden were unknown to me while right-handers Larry Jansen and Red Munger were among the guys that I had known in seasons past. This was Jansen's seventh year in the league; he was in between nine years with the New York Giants and the Cincinnati Reds. Munger was going on his seventh year in the PCL after seven years with the St. Louis Cardinals. Jack "Lucky" Lohrke was in his thirteenth year, five of which had been with the New York Giants and six in the PCL. He was a pitching infielder with the best of comical behaviors.

During this return trip into San Francisco, O'Doul reconnected with many old friends, including Walter Mails. I tried to remain inconspicuous as they told funny stories about each other. President of the Seals, Jerry Donavan, was an old buddy of O'Doul's and when the two older men came into the clubhouse together, you could cut the nostalgia with a butter knife. The season was only in its second week and Seattle would make their last trip in late August.

The next weeklong series featured the Vancouver Mounties starting on Tuesday, April 23, a night game. The local press ballyhooed the arrival as a match-up between two clubs affiliated with major league teams: the American League Boston Red Sox and the Baltimore Orioles. Vancouver's new manager was an ex-PCL major leaguer with impressive credentials, Charlie Metro. I couldn't wait to meet the man who had replaced the Great O'Doul. His work would have to be an improvement over the last-place finish in the team's first year in the league.

Trainer Hal Younkers was the first to arrive into the clubhouse and he said he was happy to see me again. He had a different look in his eyes, one that said that ending in last place again wasn't an option. It was a determination based on something he had felt in his first two weeks of the season. As the other men came in, many of whom I had known from the Oakland Oaks and a couple from Baltimore, I was under the impression that this was a team to be reckoned with.

I had a good time with infielders Johnny Jorgensen and Jim Marshall and pitchers George Bamberger, Don Ferrarese, Charlie Beamon and Fred Besana. There were a couple of guys from the San Diego Padres on this club: outfielder and coach Harry Elliott and the hardest working player in the league, infielder Buddy Peterson. Among the newcomers were third baseman Kal Segrist and outfielders Lennie Green and Joe Frazier. Of the pitchers, Erv Palica, Morrie Martin and Art Houtteman were new to me and the league.

When they got onto the field I could see why Hal Younkers felt as he did: these guys were good and they knew it. Playing for the very different Charlie Metro made them the team to watch. The week went by too fast. Before I knew it, I was saying goodbye to everyone after Sunday's doubleheader. Charlie said, "You do good work kid; see you when we come back." It was another good week for me and after the game I went to San Remo's with the Mooneys to celebrate the ballclub's productive three weeks.

The Seals traveled north to Sicks Stadium and the Seattle Rainiers, then on to Capilano Stadium, the home of the Vancouver Mounties. While they were away, I helped out more at home since both of my parents worked and there were only three of us still at home. When I wasn't occupied with domestic duties, I helped at Mrs. Troiel's shop across the street, packing ply hole covers, and continued to play on the semi-pro teams in the East Bay, first for Guy's Drugs, then for "Shoe" Hustead's ballclub.

By Monday, May 13, the Seals were back to play the Los Angeles Angels. I lugged all thirty-seven of the Angels' duffel bags into the clubhouse and spent the afternoon making things right for last year's PCL championship team. By late Tuesday afternoon my preparations were complete and I remembered Carlos Bernier reminding me that I could stay on top of almost anything with a siesta nap. I put on "Callas Portrays Puccini Heroines," by Maria Callas and drifted off until it was time to meet our rivals from the south.

It wasn't too surprising that trainer Joe Liscio would be the first of the Angels to arrive. He entered with coach Jackie Warner and we all picked up where we had left off. It was only one month into the new season and the Seals were looking good even as the Angels were holding their own. After they had won the pennant, Los Angeles made several changes, beginning with a new manager. Clay Hopper from next door's team in Hollywood replaced Bob Sheffing. Coming from the Brooklyn Dodgers organization where he had managed Montreal to a pennant in 1946 with Jackie Robinson, Clay knew baseball. Now he was getting help from the Chicago Clubs.

Like the Seals, the Angels were getting potential major leaguers from some of the best prospects in the Cubs' farm system. Clay brought another good ballclub to San Francisco led by none other than last year's PCL home-run king, Steve Bilko. Along with Steve, came George "Sparky" Anderson, a highly touted infielder who could hit with consistency. Other newcomers to the league included infielders Roy Hartsfeld and Wally Lammers, outfielders Bert Hamric and Jim Fridley, catcher Earl Battey and a host of pitchers, including a relatively new southpaw, Tommy Lasorda. From the Official Score Book, they looked powerful, fast, and in every way capable of repeating the previous year's showing. The newcomers would have to produce in the highly competitive Pacific Coast League.

An eight-game series with Sacramento began on Tuesday, May 28, and featured two doubleheaders on Memorial Day and Sunday, June 2nd. The season was nearly half over and Tommy Heath's Solons were facing a stronger Seals ballclub. Undaunted, the Solons arrived with many good players, including several returning ones. Al Heist was one of the finest outfielders in the league and had contributed a number of base hits the previous year. Infielder Harry Bright returned with similar credentials as did first baseman Nippy Jones. The three men paced the team but would have to duplicate their prior years' performances to get their club into the first division. They would also need good pitching to improve their showing. At least six men were returning, five right-handers and a southpaw: Cloyd Boyer, Milo Candini, Roger Osenbaugh, Joe Stanka, Bud Watkins, and left-hander Gene Bearden. Ex-Seal Marshall Bridges, another left-handed pitcher, along with two hurlers familiar with the PCL—ex-Oaks southpaw Roger Bowman and right-hander Earl Harris—also joined the pitching staff. Cuno Barragan and veteran Jim Mangan were the catchers.

Hitting and pitching wouldn't be enough, not in a league where major leagues were backing up many teams. A good defense was also a requirement. Al Heist, newcomer Jim Greengrass, Jimmy Westlake who had played first base, and Ed White who was new to the league would have to hold the outfield together. Nippy Jones, Harry Bright and reliable Artie Wilson took care of the infield. Tommy had all of the right horses: only time would tell if they would prove themselves first-division material.

I enjoyed working with trainer Mike Chambers and the players on this team. They were loose, had a lot of fun in the clubhouse, and were enthusiastic competitors on the field. They had heart. To me, they were the equal to the other seven teams in spite of having had their share of disappointing years and a reputation for being the league's step-child. I evaluated them on what I saw and heard in the clubhouse, not on their appearance in the standings. At the end of the eight-game series, they paid their bills and we talked about their next trip back.

The very competitive Seals spent the next two weeks on the road exhibiting good hitting and steady pitching. They went south to Gilmore Field, to go toe-to-toe with manager Clyde King's Hollywood Stars. Then, they returned north to play Sacramento at Edmonds Field. The Seals hitting had jelled into something to be reckoned with; even little Albie Pearson was connecting for hits. Paced by Frank Kellert, Marty Keough, and Bill Renna, manager Joe Gordon's team was making an interesting race. With a good defense and fair pitching, the sportswriters were scratching their heads, wondering, "What happened?"

Midway through the 1957 season, my good friend, Bill Sweeney, passed away. I hadn't been able to see him. Of all the managers in the PCL, he was the one who had taken the time to get to know me. I knew his tough exterior masked kindness. I'll never forget what he told me when he caught the batboys playing "Over the Line" with pitcher Will Hafey in 1953. "For a small fellow," he said, I would "have to give everything I had to hit the left-field fence on one or two hops." He cautioned me to not let my height interfere with my accomplishments. The look in his eyes said it all.

In my off-time, I continued to play semi-pro ball with Hustead's and go to the movies. I also made a visit to a small town north of the Bay Area, Occidental, where I heard they had fine Italian restaurants. I drove my parents there for a meal at the Union Hotel.

On Monday, June 17, the duffel bags for the San Diego Padres were delivered; after I hung up the uniforms and set the shoes out for shining, I called it a day and hightailed it over to Joe Mooney's clubhouse. He was in a good mood and offered me a beer to celebrate the Seals' good showing in the standings. He felt sure his team could go all the way if only they could get good pitching. We were several weeks away from the season's exact midpoint, the Fourth of July. Vancouver and Hollywood looked equally strong, yet just having the sensation of this much success helped us believe it could be our year. First we had to get by the farm club of the Cleveland Indians: the Padres.

Trainer Les Cook opened the door and asked, "Where's that lousy coffee we love so much?" We shook hands and I switched on the coffeemaker. He asked if I had been playing any ball. I showed him the cap I wore on Hustead's team: it looked so much like the one used by the Hollywood Stars. Then, I put on an album: "Pee Wee Hunt and his All Stars." It was almost time for the troops to arrive.

Former outfielder and infielder Bob Elliott was back for his third year as field manager, along with the club's longtime coach, Jimmie Reese. Cleveland had sent some of the brighter prospects to San Diego to see how they would fare in the toughest of the minor leagues. This was virtually a brand new ball-club with only four players returning from last year's club. Out of a roster of over thirty players, only right-handed pitcher, Pete Mesa, southpaw Vic Lombardi, outfielder Floyd Robinson, catcher Allen Jones, and third baseman Eddie Kazak were returning players who had survived the previous year's seventh-place finish. Like Boston, the Cleveland Indians didn't want another losing season from their minor leaguers; some of their hottest new prospects walked through my clubhouse door.

Second baseman Billy Moran, infielder and outfielder Rudy Regalado, shortstop Billy Harrell and outfielder Dave Pope were new to the league. Moran and Pope were high-flying stars in the Negro Leagues before owner Bill Veeck signed them to contracts with Cleveland. New to the league, Earl Averill, did most of the catching. He was son to Earl Averill, Sr., the homerun hitting Seals outfielder in the late twenties when they played at Old Rec on 15th and Valencia streets.

San Diego's pitching consisted of the every effective right-hander Mudcat Grant who at this point of the season was throwing the ball by most of the hitters. Dick Brodowski was another newbie, a right-hander who baffled hitters. The Padres also hired southpaw Hank Aguirre who quickly demonstrated his ability to get the good hitters out. All in all, manager Bob Elliott had the manpower to end up in the first division. I could tell that some would probably be called up by Cleveland near the end of the season.

The Seals battled San Diego and did okay. Like all of the teams before them, the Padres were an enthusiastic group who treated me well and showed their appreciation at the end of the Sunday doubleheader. I told Les Cook and the others that I looked forward to the last week of August when they would return.

The fans came to check out the new Seals. We hadn't had a ballclub that treated the opposition with such persuasive performances since that 1948 season when we battled the Oaks down to the finish line. They were even doing better than Tommy's 1954 Kiddee Kar Express. I was stunned by the multitudes walking up the ramp each game. Bob Freitas, the Mooneys, and I enjoyed the experience of being "a contender."

We took on Steve Bilko and the Los Angeles Angels at Wrigley Field the last week in June and all indications suggested that we were still holding our own against the Cubs' best farm club. Joe Gordon kept everybody focused on the objective and with the exception of our pitching, we continued to produce. Los Angeles was not quite the same team that they had been during the previous year when they had won the pennant sixteen games ahead of the second-place Seattle Rainiers.

For the July 4th doubleheader and a weeklong series, the Portland Beavers met the Seals in our home stadium. The revitalized Beavers battled it out with the Seals and it looked as if the teams were evenly matched. Then, we waited a week to face off with the Hollywood Stars, who were making their first appearance in San Francisco relatively late in the season. Trainer Frankie Jacobs kept his players in tip-top shape. Of the thirty men who came to town, fewer than ten were new to the league. Shortstop Leo Rodriguez, infielder Jim Baumer, and infielder and outfielder Tony Baritome arrived from the Pirates' farm system. Southpaw Don Rowe, and right-handers Bennie Daniels and George Witt were also from the Pirate organization and first-time PCL players.

Among the returning players was my nemesis, Carlos Bernier. I greeted him using as much Spanish as I knew: "Buenas dias, mi nombre es Guillermo Soto. Yo soy Mexicano." (Good day, my name is William Soto. I am Mexican.) He smiled and rattled off several colorful expressions in less than a minute. I could tell he was pleased with my efforts. Other returning players included outfielders Bill Causion and Paul Pettit and second baseman Spook Jacobs. Among the eight pitchers coming back were Curt Raydon, Ben Wade, Bob Garber, Chuck Churn, and Laurin Pepper. This was a good ballclub, but by midseason it came down to which major league team would put up the money to gain the personnel that could succeed. Baltimore, Boston, and Pittsburgh were all exerting their influence.

Before the Stars left town, I took Bernier to the Mission District, San Francisco's mostly Spanish-speaking neighborhoods. He talked with local merchants in Spanish; as they looked over at me, they scratched their chins and smiled. Some players on opposing teams accused Bernier of being a show-boat, just full of himself. The local press didn't like him enough to give him an opportunity to ever explain himself. Tempestuous Carlos—a terror on the base-paths—but an okay guy in how he treated me.

The Seals gave Hollywood a rude welcome. For seven seasons, Hollywood and Seattle had dominated the league, and the Seals had been the "also rans." In 1957, things were truly different.

With the exception of the Portland Beavers, the remaining six visiting teams would return only one more time before the close of the season. The front office brass must have felt proud as the big crowds poured in. Bob Freitas, Joe and Nancy Mooney, Chico Norton, and I spent the rest of the season watching the Seals succeed. The hitters were hitting, especially outfielders Bill Renna and Albie Pearson, infielder Grady Hatton, and second baseman Ken Aspromonte.

Manager Joe Gordon received more than adequate defense from the infield, the outfield and the catchers. Only the pitching was questionable. Most of the season's starting pitchers had difficulty holding on to leads, no matter the spread. One guy came through with consistency, however, relief pitcher Leo Kiley, a leftie. As the season wound down to its final weeks, the Seals and Vancouver were battling it out toward the September 15 double-header. Even if we lost both games to the visiting Sacramento Solons, we still would win the pennant. Imagine that.

By late August and into early September, the newspapers were talking about major league baseball coming to San Francisco. For me and for many of the people I knew, it had always been here. The Red Sox put the icing on the top and gave us some bright prospects. We had a better ballpark than many in the major leagues and had an attendance record to celebrate. I had a feeling that the Red Sox would open the doors to the American League for San Francisco.

When we clinched the pennant on that last day of the season, the Sacramento ballplayers and Tommy Heath acknowledged Joe Gordon for the good job he had done. The fans were treated to a great day as the managers of both teams took it to the batter's box to hit one out. Everybody was loose: the Seals had won the pennant and the fans enjoyed the moment.

After the players departed, I cleaned the clubhouse, gathered the used towels for the laundry man, and removed any unsold products from the General Store. I headed over to the Seals Clubhouse where trainer Leo Hughes and Joe Mooney were at the tail-end of a long overdue celebration. I congratulated as many of the guys who were still there and shared a beer with Joe and Bob Freitas. Leo Hughes had an almost forlorn look in his eyes. I couldn't tell if it was the beer or his memories of eleven years earlier when we had last taken the pennant.

SAN FRANCISCO (SEALS) BAY AREA BASEBALL CLUB

Bottom Row: L to R—TOM HURD, P; SAL TAORMINA, O F; BILL ABERNATHIE, P; JOE GORDON, Mgr.; GLENN WRIGHT, Coach; NINI TORNAY, C; HARRY DORISH, P; KEN ASPROMONTE, 2nd B.

2nd Row: L to R—LEO HUGHES, Trainer; BILL PROUT, P; JACK SPRING, P; LEO KIELY, P; FRANK KELLERT, 1st B; HAYWOOD SULLIVAN, C; BILL RENNA, O F; ED SADOWSKI, C; ALBIE PIERSON, O F.

Top Row: L to R—GRADY HATTON, 3rd B; R. W. SMITH, P; BERT THIEL, P; JACK PHILLIPS, Inf; MARTY KEOUGH, O F; TOM UMPHLETT, O F; ROBERT CHAKALES, P; HARRY MALMBERG, S S.

The 1957 pennant-winning San Francisco Seals

There was talk of a victory celebration at a restaurant downtown. I headed back to the other side of the Bay, slightly euphoric from my one beer. I kept remembering how this adventure had started out, about Damon Miller and his letter telling me to show up to Seals Stadium for the first time as a batboy. I kept thinking about that little sign near Leo's rubbing table: "You're through when you quit trying."

Coda

The House I Lived in

Seals Stadium was my home away from home. I sought refuge there whenever it was convenient. After the September 15th double-header and winning the pennant for the first time since 1946, I learned about the double-cross: Mayor Christopher, major league baseball, and the big shots who ran the victorious Seals out of San Francisco. It was the end of the plan by the Boston Red Sox to bring the Seals into the American League. It was the end for the part of my life lived in the House of Baseball. While I knew I could adjust to an unknown future, what was the prospect for the San Francisco Seals? In the empty clubhouse I recalled that music soothes the savage beast and so I refer to songwriter Lewis Allen with quotes from one of his best songs: "The House I Live In." Recorded during World War II, it asked "What is America to me?"

" . . . The house I live in . . . "

After so many Friday nights spent sleeping over in the First Aid Station, and then living through an entire winter there in 1956, Seals Stadium was truly my other residence. I was safely home in the Emerald Cathedral.

Mooney and I occupied one of three "club rooms." We lived in what had once been the locker room of San Francisco's second professional club, the

From "SHORT FILM"

THE HOUSE I LIVE IN

(That's America To Me)

Words by
LEWIS ALLAN

Music by
EARL ROBINSON

Mission Bears, later renamed the Mission Reds. The kitchen where we cooked our meals had been a covey of lockers and our temporary quarters—only a couple of decades earlier—had been the dressing room for many of the era's most notable athletes.

Legendary outfielder and hitting sensation, Ox Eckhardt, banged out 275 hits in the ball park's first year in business in 1931. Because of the stadium's design, the outfield fences were beyond the reach of even the best power hitters, thus limiting his home runs to seven. Eckhardt's teammates in the outfield included Jimmy Welsh and Bud Hafey, the first of three brothers to play in the league. (Tom Hafey would eventually come along to play for the Oakland Oaks and Los Angeles while Will Hafey played for the Oaks, the Seals, and San Diego).

" . . . The place I work in, the worker at my side. . . ."

Buzzy Casazza and Bobby Rodriguez

In my first season on the field, I worked with Don Rode, Buzzy Casazza and Bob Rodriguez. In subsequent years, I worked with Bobby Ferguson, Frankie Donofrio, and Johnny McCormack. We were teenagers, full of enthusiasm and the willingness to work hard for a major league operation. There wasn't a prima donna among us. We did what we were told and what was expected of us, always under the watchful eyes of our supervisors, Don Rode and Leo Hughes. The ballplayers from both dugouts taught us by example to accept and respect one another no matter who we were or where we came from; it was the unimagined benefit of working in an integrated Pacific Coast League.

I failed to realize that a batboy's tenure ends when he graduates from high school. It was my good fortune (or was it luck?) that Don Rode offered me the job of running the Visitors clubhouse. Otherwise, my employment with the Seals would have ended on June 18, 1954. Branch Rickey was right when he said "luck is the residue of design."

In the locker room, I worked side-by-side with all of the leagues' visiting trainers, each possessing a special work ethic. I learned that life is utterly useless without a sense of humor. By working alongside Chico Norton, supervisor of the janitorial crew, and his team, I greatly improved my housekeeping skills. I maintained a special working relationship with the Seals' clubhouse men as well. Don Rode left the Seals in 1956 to forge a career with Pacific Telephone. Then the Boston Red Sox took over the franchise in 1956 and brought a major league work ethic in the form and character of Joe Mooney and business manager Bob Freitas. Both were hands-on, hard-working men. For the first time, I had a direct working relationship with management which turned out to be both positive and rewarding.

There were countless others who worked to make the ball club the major league organization that it was and I hope my story has given them their just credit.

" . . . The little corner newsstand, the house a mile tall . . . "

At the corner of 16th & Bryant, there were two newsstands. One took up residence in front of Stanfel's Double Play Cocktail Lounge. On a clear and sunny day you could watch the fans approach the stadium's front gates. After lunch, I often walked out of the place, rubbed my eyes and looked straight ahead at the majestic outline created by the stadium. Before crossing the street, I could see the first-base side of the ball park descend Bryant Street towards the bakery which stood on one side of the street with Hamm's Brewery opposite.

The other newsstand stood sentinel in front of a Greek-owned diner. Later, it was called The Third Base. Next to it was a smoke shop where newspapers and tobacco attracted ballplayers and fans alike. You could walk out in front of both establishments and see not one but two "mile-high" establishments: Hamm's Brewery and the Stadium.

" . . . The town I live in, the street, the house, the room . . . "

San Francisco in the fall of 1957: what a beautiful city! Whenever I wanted to get the full flavor of a moment, I left the clubhouse and walked up the center section behind home to the press box. If it was unlocked, I placed myself at the narrow table in front of the glass window to enjoy a full view. It was breathtaking; beyond the left and center field fences was the City. San Francisco's Potrero District was a repository of light and heavy industry factories that turned out a variety of products. It had been the residential area where my relatives lived on Vermont Street. Its freeway exit dropped you off Highway 101 to Seals Stadium.

Potrero Avenue ran parallel to the left-field fence and led to downtown at its north end and toward San Francisco General Hospital to the south. Bryant Street ran parallel behind the Visitors clubhouse. Here several small businesses, industries and modest one and two-story houses coexisted, including the home belonging to my mother's Aunt Lola. Beyond Bryant and all the way to 24th and Treat was where my family lived before we moved to Oakland and West Berkeley. I was four. Down 16th Street, you would find Kilpatrick's warehouse, several grocery stores, and some small diners. Eventually you reached South Van Ness Avenue, Mission Street, and the hills heading toward Golden Gate Park and the Pacific Ocean.

"... But especially the people, that's America to me ..."

This adventure proved to me that the kindness of people can be overwhelming. West Berkeley set the tone. I witnessed the men in our community going out of their way to help a kid step up to any situation. It was pure luck to grow up in West Berkeley, in the company of kids of every ethnic persuasion. We had very little but the friendships we developed on the playgrounds, at the YMCA, in two city parks and in a nearby recreation hall, lasted lifetimes. Our commonality was baseball, yet we played any and all indoor and outdoor games. Many of those early friendships persist in the form of the Berkeley Senior Yellow Jackets, the Berkeley Breakfast Club, the Berkeley Alumni Association (alumni of the Berkeley Public Schools), and other local civic and community organizations.

Damon Miller helped me take that first step into the Seals Clubhouse. I was never able to tell him how grateful I was for his invitation. Instead, when I met his widow Kay at the 1994 Seals Stadium Reunion I made it clear how much it had meant to me. Everybody on and off the playing field and in both dugouts brought some measure of goodness into my life.

People were considerate in the 1950s, no matter where I happened to find myself. For half the decade, I spent hours on public transportation, in neighborhood bars, diners and coffee shops, where I listened to locals talk proudly about the Seals. For those early years when I didn't have a car, the bus and Key

System drivers showed concern about their passengers. Maybe it was me, the way I gravitated towards people, hopeful that I would be treated okay, but I never did run into a bully or a chronic malcontent along the way. The closest I got to mob violence was on those rare afternoons when the ball park crowd disagreed with an umpire's decision and waved their handkerchiefs or threw their seat cushions on the field forcing the umpire to halt the game.

The people I met seemed to possess a pride in their work. They worked hard for the Seals because we were a first class, big league organization. It seemed to be our unspoken mantra. We reached our zenith when the Boston Red Sox took over the franchise in 1956, fell flat on their faces only to lift themselves off the floor and win the '57 pennant!

During their last seven seasons in San Francisco, the Seals expanded my knowledge beyond my wildest dreams. I learned to be tolerant, cordial and humorous, while developing a strong work ethic.

Like those colorful men in both dugouts for whom I worked, I had many good seasons and a few bad ones, hitting streaks followed by slumps, and I made a few errors along the way, but most importantly, I also got in some good plays.

H. J. Brunnier, structural engineer who designed Seals Stadium, watching the end of his dream

Bibliography

Minor League Baseball

Blake, Mike. *The Minor Leagues: A Celebration of the Big Show*. (Linwood Press, New York, NY: 1991).

Byan, Bob. *Wait 'til I Make the Show: Baseball in the Minor Leagues*. (Sports Illustrated, Little Brown & Co., Boston, MA: 1974).

Chadwick, Bruce. *Baseball's Home Town Teams: The Story of the Minor Leagues*. (Abberville Press, New York, NY: 1994).

Finch, Addington, and Morgan. *The Story of Minor League Baseball*. (National Association of Professional Baseball Leagues, 1953).

Johnson, Lloyd, and Wolff, Miles. *The Encylcopedia of Minor League Baseball*. (Baseball America, Durham, NC: 1993).

Johnson, Lloyd, and Wolff, Miles. *The Encyclopedias of Minor League Baseball, 2nd Edition*. (Baseball America, Durham, NC: 1997).

Johnson, Lloyd. *The Minor League Registar*. (Baseball America, Durham, NC: 1994).

Lamb, David. *Stolen Season: A Journey Through America and Baseball's Minor Leagues*. (Random House, New York, NY: 1991).

Nelson, Kevin. *The Golden Game: The Story of California Baseball*. (California Historic Society Press, San Francisco, CA: 2004).

Obojdki, Robert. *Bush League: A Colorful, Factual Account of Minor League Baseball from 1877 to Present*. (MacMillan, New York, NY: 1975).

Reinhardt, Bryson, with Nagel, Walter. *Five Straight Errors on Ladies Day*. (Claxton Press, Caldwell, ID: 1965).

Sullivan, Neil J. *The Minors*. (St. Martin's Press, New York, NY: 1990).

Weiss, Bill and Wright, Marshall. *The 100 Greatest Minor League Baseball Teams of the 20th Century*. (Outskirts Press, 2006).

Wright, Marshall. *The American Association: Year By Year Stats 1902-1952*. (McFarland & Co., Jefferson, NC: 1997).

Wright, Marshall. *The International League: Year by Year Stats 1884-1953*. (McFarland & Co., Jefferson, NC: 1998).

West Coast Baseball

Bauer, Carlos. *The Coast League Cyclopedia: An Encyclopedia of the Old Pacific Coast League, 1903-57, 3 volumes*. (Baseball Press Books, San Diego & San Marino, CA, 2003).

Bauer, Carlos. *The Early Coast League Statistical Record, 1903-57*. (Baseball Press Books, San Diego, CA, 2004).

Beverage, Richard. *The Angels: L.A. in the P.C.L., 1919-1957*. (Deacon Press, Los Angeles, CA: 1981).

Beverage, Richard. *The Hollywood Stars: Baseball in Movieland, 1926-1957*. (Deacon Press, Los Angeles, CA 1984).

Carlson, Kip, and Anderson, Paul. *Portland Beavers*. (Images of Baseball, Arcadia Press, Charleston, SC: 2004).

Dobbins, Dick, and Twitchell, John. *Nuggets on the Diamond: Professional Baseball in the Bay Area from the Gold Rush to the Present*. (Woodford Press, San Francisco, CA: 1994).

Jacobs, Martin, and McGuire, Jack. *The San Francisco Seals*. (Images of Baseball, Arcadia Press, Charleston, SC: 2005).

Jordan, Jacob. *Six Seasons: A History of the Tacoma Giants, 1960-1965*. (Green Dragon Publishing, Tacoma, WA: 1996).

Kelly, Brent. *The San Francisco Seals, 1946-1957. Interviews with Twenty-Five Former Baseballers*. (McFarland & Co., Jefferson, NC: 2002).

Leutzinger, Richard. *Lefty O'Doul: The Legend that Baseball Almost Forgot*. (Carmel Bay Press, Carmel, CA: 1997).

Mackey, Scott. *Barbary Baseball: The P.C.L. of the 20's*. (McFarland & Co., Jefferson, NC: 1995).

Medeiros, Mark D., and Zinger, Paul, J. *Runs, Hits and an Era: The Pacific Coast League: 1903-1958*. (University of Illinois Press, Urbana, IL: 1994).

O'Neal, Bill. *The P.C.L. 1903-1988*. (Eakin Press, Austin, TX: 1990).

McWilliams, Doug. *Pacific Coast League News, May 14, 1946—May 10, 1951. A Complete Reprint.* (Republished by Doug McWilliams, in honor of the P.C.L.'s 100th Annniversary; Berkeley, CA: 2002).

Runquist Willie. *P.C.L. Almanac, 16 volumes, 1938-1953.* (Published by Willie Runquist, British Columbia, Canada, annually).

Runquist, Willie. *A Heavenly Series: The Hollywood Stars Versus the Los Angeles Angels, 1938-1957.* (Published by Willie Runquist, British Columbia, Canada.

Snelling, Dennis. *The P.C.L.: A Statistical History, 1903-1957.* (McFarland & Co., Jefferson, NC: 1995).

Snelling, Dennis. *Supplement to The P.C.L. A Statistical History.* (McFarland & Co., Jefferson, NC.

Spalding, John. *Always on Sunday, The California League: 1886-1915.* (Ag Press, Manhattan, KS: 1992).

Spalding, John. *P.C.L. Stars, 100 of the Best 1903-1957, Volume 1.* (Ag Press, Manhattan, KS: 1994).

Spalding, John. *P.C.L. Trivia Book, Facts about Fabulous Feats and Foolishness: 1903-1957.* (Published by John Spalding, San Jose, CA: 1997).

Stadler, Ken. *The P.C.L.: One Man's Memories, 1938-1957.* (Marbeck Publications, Los Angeles, CA: 1984).

Swank, William G., and Smith III, James D. *This Was Paradise: Voices of the P.C.L. Padres 1936-1958,* bound reprint from *The Journal of San Diego History,* Vol. 41, #1, Winter 1995 (San Diego Historical Society, San Diego, CA: 1995).

Swank, William, and Brandes, Ray. *Lane Field Padres, 2 volumes.* (San Diego Padres and the San Diego Baseball Historical Society, San Diego, CA: 1997).

Swank, Bill. *Echoes from Lane Field: The History of the San Diego Padres, 1936-1957.* (Turner Publishing, Paducah, KY: 1997).

Swank, Bill. *Baseball in San Diegoe: From Padres to Petco.* (Images of Baseball, Arcadia Press, Charleston, SC: 2004).

Waddingham, Gary. *The Seattle Rainiers 1935-42.* (Writers Publishing Service, Seattle, WA: 1987).

Wells, Donald. *The Race for the Governor's Cup: The P.C.L. Playoffs 1936-1954.* (McFarland & Co., Jefferson, NC: 2000).

Wells, Donald. *Baseball's Western Front: The P.C.L. During WWII.* (McFarland & Co., Jefferson, NC: 2004).

Appendix A

Hit Songs in the Years I Worked for the San Francisco Seals

1951

Because of You, *Tony Bennett*
Be My Love, *Mario Lanza*
Come On-a My House,
    Rosemary Clooney
Cry, *Johnnie Ray and the Four Lads*
Detour, *Patti Page*
Have Mercy Baby, *Billy Ward, Dominos*
Louisiana Blues, *Muddy Waters*
My Heart Cries For You, *Guy Mitchell*
Sixty Minute Man,
    Billy Ward, Dominoes
Too Young, *Nat King Cole*

1952

Blues in the Night, *Rosemary Clooney*
Glow Worm, *The Mills Brothers*
Heart and Soul, *The Four Aces*
Here is my Heart, *Al Martino*
High Noon, *Frankie Laine*
Kiss of Fire, *Georgia Gibbs*
Maybe, *Perry Como and Eddie Fisher*
Tenderly, *Rosemary Clooney*
Till I Waltz again with You,
    Teresa Brewer
Unforgettable, *Nat King Cole*

1953

Crying in the Chapel, *The Orioles*
I Believe, *Frankie Laine*
I've Got the World on a String,
Frank Sinatra,
Pretend, *Nat King Cole*
P.S. I Love You, *The Hilltoppers*
Stranger in Paradise, *Tony Bennett*
Vaya Con Dios, *Les Paul and Mary Ford*
Changing Partners, *Patti Page*
Song from Moulin Rouge, *Percy Faith*
That's Amore, *Dean Martin*

1954

Answer Me My Love, *Nat King Cole*
Cross Over the Bridge, *Patti Page*
If I Give My Heart to You, *Doris Day*
Hey There, *Rosemary Clooney*
Make Love to Me, *Jo Stafford*
Secret Love, *Doris Day*
This Ole House, *Rosemary Clooney*
Three Coins in the Fountain, *Four Aces*
Wanted, *Perry Como*
Young at Heart, *Frank Sinatra*

1955

Maybellene, *Chuck Berry*
Rock Around the Clock, *Bill Haley*
Tutti Frutti, *Little Richard*
Speedoo, *The Cadillacs*
The Great Pretender, *The Platters*
At My Front Door, *The El Dorados*
When You Dance, *The Turbans*
Ain't That a Shame, *Fats Domino*
I Hear You Knockin', *Smiley Lewis*
Pledging My Love, *Johnny Ace*

1956

Hound Dog, Don't be Cruel,
    Elvis Presley
Roll Over Beethoven, *Chuck Berry*
In the Still of the Nite,
    The Five Satins
Long Tall Sally, *Little Richard*
Blueberry Hill, *Fats Domino*
Blue Suede Shoes, *Carl Perkins*
Why Do Fools Fall in Love,
    Frankie Lyman
I Walk the Line, *Johnny Cash*
Honky Tonk, Part 2, *Bill Doggett*

1957

Whole Lotta Shakin' Going On,
    Jerry Lee Lewis
Jailhouse Rock, *Elvis Presley*
Peggy Sue, *Buddy Holly*
You Send Me, *Sam Cooke*
Come Go With Me, *The Del-Vikings*
School Days, *Chuck Berry*
Lucille, *Little Richard*
Little Darlin', *The Diamonds*
Blue Monday, *Fats Domino*
Wake Up Little Suzie,
    The Everly Brothers

Hit Movies in the Years I Worked for the San Francisco Seals

1951

The African Queen, J. Huston

Alice in Wonderland, Disney Studios

An American in Paris, V. Minelli

A Christmas Carol, B. D. Hurst

The Day the Earth Stood Still, R. Wise

The Lavender Hill Mob, C. Crichton

A Place in the Sun, G. Stevens

Stranger on a Train, A. Hitchcock

A Streetcar Named Desire, E. Kazan

1952

The Bad and the Beautiful, V. Minelli

Come Back Little Sheba, D. Mann

The Crimson Pirate, R. Siodmak

Death of a Salesman, L. Benedek

Five Fingers, J. L. Mankiewicz

The Greatest Show On Earth,
    C.B. DeMille

High Noon, F. Zinnmann

Moulin Rouge, J. Huston

Pat and Mike, G. Cukor

The Quiet Man, J. Ford

Singin' in the Rain, G Kelly, S. Donan

Viva Zapata, E. Kazan

1953

The Band Wagon, V. Minelli

Them Big Heat, F. Lang

From Here to Eternity, F. Zinnemann

Julius Caesar, J. L. Mankiewicz

The Robe, H. Koster

Roman Holiday, W. Wyler

Shane, G. Stevens

Stalag 17, B. Wilder

Titanic, J. Negulesco

War of the Worlds, B. Haskin

The Wild One, L. Benedek

1954

The Caine Mutiny, E. Dymtryk

The Country Girl, G. Seaton

Dial M for Murder, A. Hitchcock

Johnny Guitar, N. Ray

On the Waterfront, E. Kazan

Rear Window, A. Hitchcock

Sabrina, B .Wilder

Seven Brides for Seven Brothers,
    S. Donen

A Star Is Born, G. Cukor

Them, G. Douglas

1955

Bad Day at Black Rock, J. Sturges
The Blackboard Jungle, R. Brooks
East of Eden, E. Kazan
Kiss Me Deadly, R. Aldrich
Lady and the Tramp, Disney Studio
Marty, D. Mann
Mister Roberts, J. Ford
The Night of the Hunter, C. Laughton
Picnic, J. Logan

1956

Anastasia, A. Litvak
Around the World in 80 Days,
    M. Anderson
Baby Doll, E. Kazan
Bus Stop, J. Logan
Carousel, H. King
Forbidden Planet, F. McLeod Wilcox
Friendly Persuasion, W. Wilder
Giant, G. Stevens
Invasion of the Body Snatchers, D. Siegel
The King and I, W. Lang
Lust for Life, V. Minelli
The Man Who Knew Too Much,
    A. Hitchcock
Moby Dick, J. Huston
The Searchers, J. Ford
The Ten Commandments, C. B. DeMille
Written on the Wind, D. Sirk

1957

The Bridge on the River Kwai, D. Lean
A Face in the Crowd, E. Kazan
Funny Face, S. Donen
Gunfight at the O.K. Corral, J. Sturges
The Incredible Shrinking Man, J. Arnold
Jailhouse Rock, R. Thorpe
The Pajama Game, G. Abbott, S Donen
Paths of Glory, S. Kubrick
Peyton Place, M. Robson
Sayonara, J. Logan
The Spirit of St. Louis, B. Wilder
Sweet Smell of Success, A. MacKendrick
The Three Faces of Eve, N. Johnson
12 Angry Men, S. Lumet
Witness for the Prosecution, B. Wilder

About the Author

A fourth generation San Franciscan, Bill Soto-Castellanos grew up in the same West Berkeley neighborhood of Augie Galan, Emil Maihlo, and Billy Martin. At age 15, while attending Burbank Junior High School in West Berkeley, he went to work for the San Francisco Seals baseball club. From Visitors batboy to Seals ballboy to the Visiting team's clubhouse man, Soto-Castellanos worked with the franchise during their last seven seasons in the old Pacific Coast League. He went on to a career in Labor Relations, retiring in 2000 to write *16th & Bryant*. He was married to the late Alicia Corella for 57 years, had one daughter, Gina-Monique, and a grandson, Luis-Antonio. Bill lives in Pinole, CA.